Sign of the End

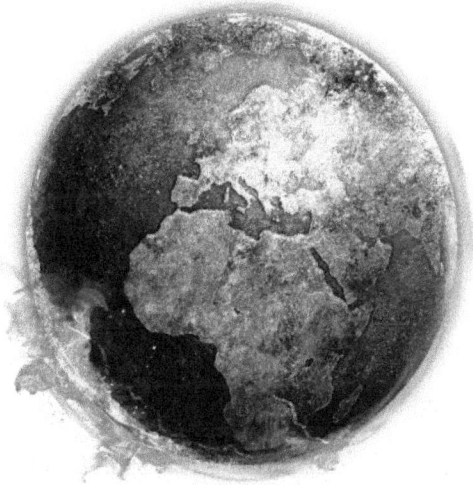

Thomas A. Bentley

Sign of the End

Other Works by the same author

Reformation 2.0 – The Next Move for God's People

Surviving Science

How to Think about Science in the Age of Evolution

Have you Swallowed the Hook?

Table of Contents

The last indignation is the proclamation that God is not the Creator of life, and the Bible is not to be followed anymore.

The world is sitting on the cusp of dramatic change. Time is short.

The purpose of this book is to outline what is coming upon the earth. The two main sources will be prophecy and history, and both are going to illustrate that time is shorter than you think. The world is preparing itself for a battle with the Almighty. Little do they know, God is preparing to use these changes, just as God used the nations of old, in the working out of His purposes.

The last indignation is coming. Are you ready to meet it?

Chapter 1

Introduction

Have you ever waited for anything? One summer when I was a teenager, I experienced the longest wait of my young life. It was an amusement park ride that had just opened. It was billed as a thrill ride that rivaled the meanest rollercoasters around. As you could imagine, the line started almost at the entrance of the park. That's where I started to wait. I couldn't even see the ride itself, but an hour later I was nearing the place where I could glimpse the top of the building. Forty-five minutes later I neared the serpentine crowd control area. Finally, after two hours it was my turn. Sitting in the seat, and watching the safety bar go down, I realized that there was no turning back – the wait was over.

Waiting for the second coming of Jesus Christ can feel like that. Humanity is coming up on the two-thousand-year mark in its wait for the promised return. How near are we to the end? How can you know? One Christian sect claims that you can't know, that there are no mileposts for us to look at today, that there is nothing available to us so that we can discern the times we are living. Another Christian sect believes we are already living in a realized coming of Christ. They see the visible structure of their church becoming politically more connected and influential with the governments of the world. For them, that is the City of God, conquering the world and ushering in a golden age. Still others take a different approach. Following Origen, the early church father and master of allegorizing the scriptures (Brown, 86), this group has decided the second coming should be seen spiritually as something that happens inside the believer. In recent years, this spiritualized coming of Christ has been manifested by using the meditation techniques of mystic eastern religions. There are many Christian authors today who teach these methods of emptying the mind to search for the god inside. What if there was another way?

What if Jesus did leave milestones, signs that help biblical followers of Christ to discern the times they are living? It turns out that Jesus did provide many signs. One of them was a warning not to follow after anyone on this earth claiming to be Jesus (Matthew 24:4-26). Within this section of scripture, Jesus revealed specific birth pains that would grow as the time neared. One specific sign, is an increase in lawlessness. Seeing criminality, and watching people commit crimes without consequences, will cause good people to stop caring. Paul also gave the church a specific sign. He stated that unless this sign happened literally in history, the second coming will not occur (1 Thessalonians 4). It turns out that there really are mileposts we can discern while we are waiting. Just as in my wait to ride the rollercoaster, mileposts can be found in Bible prophecy. When I saw the top of the building, I could gage how close I was. When I saw the serpentine crowd control area, I knew I was closer. In the same way, there are signs in Bible prophecy that you need to discover. Helping you do that is the purpose of this book.

It is a sad commentary that most Christians today do not know much about Bible prophecy. What they do know has been heavily filtered. Authoritarian figures from the past have inserted their own beliefs and ideas on how to interpret Bible prophecy so that it has no connection with us today. They have masked the plain meaning of the texts with allegory. They have broken the symmetry and beauty of how these prophecies have been put together. The result is confusion. Fortunately, there is a way to discover these milestones through Bible prophecy.

I suggest we go on a journey. A guided tour of biblical lands. Let's explore the prophecies of Daniel and its connections to the book of Revelation. In this tour you will begin to see milestones that have been intentionally placed into the prophetic landscape of human history; ones that will reveal why we have been waiting so long for the return of Christ. In this discovery we will let the Bible interpret itself, and then look into the pages of history to see if these things are so. The result of this simple approach will yield a landscape of prophetic history revealed. For some this will be difficult.

There are many that really need to go on this exploration with me, but they are saddled with baggage from their experience with popular Christianity. If you are a secularist, or a person who has grown up in the popular churches of today, this will all seem strange. What you have been taught to believe has always been fed you through the lens of another's interpretation. Not many have let the beauty, and the symmetry of what God has inspired simply speak for itself. I propose that we do this together, and friends, there is an urgency.

The prophecies in both Daniel and the Revelation, can help you see the world you are living in today in a new light. Our world is being prepared. Systems are being set up today, and when they are fully in place they will play a part in earths final events right before Jesus returns. Wouldn't you like to know what to look for? There are signs imbedded in these prophecies that unlock the meaning of today's world. Understanding these signs will prevent you from picking the wrong side when the end does come crashing down around you. The people of the earth are nearing the time when they will take their seats in the last rollercoaster ride. You don't want to be strapped in and going up the first hill only to see that you chose the wrong rollercoaster. How can you be certain? Study Bible prophecy.

Before we look at the sign of the end, the battle of Armageddon, and the shape the world will take before Jesus returns, we need to study Daniel and how it connects with the book of Revelation. This is what we will do first. Next, we will explore that the Bible says about the second coming. That will propel us into the sign of the end, Armageddon, and the world on fire. I pray that your journey is free from the speed bumps of presuppositions. Let's approach the scriptures as little children, seeking for God to reveal to us the inspired messages they hold.

In this journey I recommend that you choose a Bible that uses a word for word translation strategy, instead of a paraphrase style of interpretation. This will enable you to see more clearly the symmetry, and beauty of what God has inspired. I will be using the King James Version, the New King James Version, and the English Standard Version.

As you start, prayerfully approach the inspired text. Are you ready? Let's go.

Chapter 2

Understanding Daniel & Revelation

To understand Daniel and how Daniel's prophecy intersects with Revelation, read Daniel 2. That chapter contains the dream God gives a pagan king to show him what will come after him. This dream will become for us a guide for unpacking the prophecies in Daniel 7; Daniel 8-9; and Daniel 10-12.

READ DANIEL 2.

Seriously, get your Bible, look in the table of contents for the Old Testament prophet Daniel; sit down, and read the chapter. It won't take long. What follows is a summary of what God reveals to Daniel. I have taken the metal man and outlined it as a chart with the vertical axis representing time, and next to it the historical kingdom that each metal represents (See Figure 1).

We find that this metal man is actually a timeline. Its different metals representing different kingdoms that will arise upon the earth. All of these kingdoms are located around the great sea which is the Mediterranean Sea. All of the action in Daniel is centered around this great sea. Isn't it amazing that all of this was known in Daniel's day. The book of Daniel was found among the famous Dead Sea Scrolls. It was found to be written in the script style used at the time he wrote it. Amazing! In case you are wondering, how do I know what kingdoms came after Babylon? We know historically and from archaeology.

That is how I get the dates for these kingdoms. Second, as we continue studying further in Daniel, we will find angel interpreters who actually name some of these kingdoms. This solidifies this historical methodology. I will not be using any allegorical or other forced interpretations in this study.

Daniel 2 Summary Chart

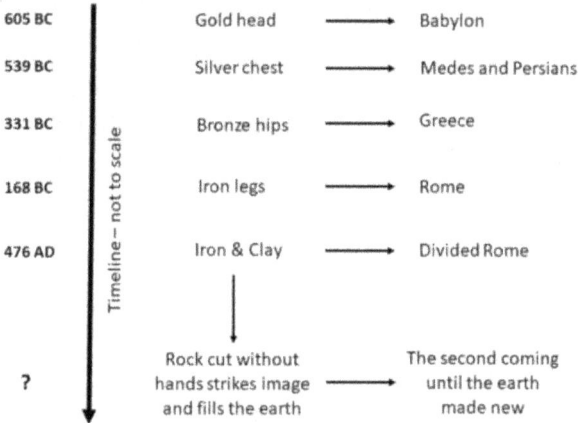

605 BC	Gold head	→	Babylon
539 BC	Silver chest	→	Medes and Persians
331 BC	Bronze hips	→	Greece
168 BC	Iron legs	→	Rome
476 AD	Iron & Clay	→	Divided Rome
?	Rock cut without hands strikes image and fills the earth	→	The second coming until the earth made new

Timeline – not to scale

Figure 1.

Also, did you notice that the timeline is unbroken. I mention this because one of the methods that prophetic interpreters use today is called Preterism. Under this belief, you claim that all prophecy must be fulfilled in the day of the prophet. It was invented by a counter reformation Jesuit named Luis de Alcazar (1554-1613). The motivation was to take prophecies that speak of the Antichrist, the little horn, the sea beast, or otherwise points to the papacy in history, and deny the association by claiming that it all had to be fulfilled in the first century. This form of interpretation is popular with Protestant Christian groups who have chosen to believe in Darwinian Evolution. Using this method is part of a larger higher criticism of the miracles in the Bible, and the historicity of the texts. However, notice that Daniel 2 has an unbroken history that begins in his day and continues long past the first century. Every prophecy in the book of Daniel is linear like this. They fill the pages of history and cannot be relegated to some period in the past. It is interesting that the very first fossil fake was also attended by a Jesuit. The fake was the Piltdown Man and the Jesuit was Pierre Teilhard de Chardin. This fossil fake tricked the world into believing in Darwinian Evolution. It was shown to be a fake 40 years too late. It truly changed the course of the world.

The fact that the timeline is unbroken also refutes the most popular method used today by conservative Protestants in interpreting Daniel's prophecies. This method is called Dispensational Futurism. It was popularized by a Protestant named John Nelson Darby, who was associated with a group in England called the Plymouth Brethren around the year 1832. Historian, E. R. Sandeen, who writes about this period, indicates that this group was largely filled with futurists. He writes; "The Futurists believed that none of the events predicted in Revelation (following the first three introductory chapters), had yet occurred, and that they would not occur until the end of this dispensation" (Sandeen, 37). Doing this, of course, breaks the harmony of the book of Revelation, and results in fanciful interpretations. It turns out that this idea was not their own, but could be traced back to a counter reformation Jesuit. Sandeen remarks: "The futurist position did not originate with the Plymouth Brethren. Sixteenth-century Roman Catholic commentators had countered Protestant attacks upon the papacy as the Antichrist by insisting that none of the events relating to Antichrist had yet occurred" (Sandeen 37). It was Lacunza's *Coming of Messiah in Glory and*

Majesty (1827), the work of the Spanish Jesuit who invented this idea, and it was brought forward via a Protestant named Irving, who translated the work.

The entire goal of futurism is to distort the prophecies and to hide what they say about the historical acts of the papacy. Darby was influential in getting the Plymouth Brethren to adopt this view. Sandeen writes that to solidify his futurist views, Darby also brought into discussion with the Plymouth Brethren another new idea, a secret rapture of Jesus, and something even more astonishing, a breaking of the historicity of time prophecies. Darby chose to break the linear history found in a time prophecy of Daniel 9. To justify this he invented a secret second coming of Christ and claimed that time would continue on earth after the secret coming leaving the last seven years of the time prophecy in Daniel 9. This break between the sixty-ninth and seventieth weeks of Daniel 9 becomes for Darby a new Christian dispensation (Sandeen, 38).

These inventions are the basis behind the theology of dispensationalism. A word that takes its meaning for how people are saved differently at different times. For example, today's disciples of Darby have come up with three dispensations, the folks in the Old Testament saved by works, the current Church age before the secret rapture by grace, and a third dispensation after the rapture. By cutting up the historicity of the 490-year time prophecy in Daniel 9, Darby created what he believed to be a final dispensation that he says will begin after his secret second coming of Jesus. This third dispensation now becomes a third period prior to a third coming of Christ. It is this period that fills the fictional books in the Left Behind series. In this final dispensation people going through the tribulation are seen as being able have a second chance.

This idea, created by Darby, that people are saved differently in different eras has created some strange theology.

My Bible tells me that everyone who is saved in the end, regardless of when they lived, will be saved by Jesus and what He did on the Cross. No one who is in Heaven will be there for any other reason than the grace provided by the Son of God. (See Hebrews 9:11-15, especially verse 15, which categorically states that Jesus' death on the cross provided redemption for sin under the first covenant.) (See also, Hebrew 11-12 and Genesis 3:15).

The implications of following the Jesuit interpretation of futurism and then adding this secret rapture would turn out to be immense. First, claiming that the prophetic time table has been interrupted, Darby taught that all unfulfilled prophecies belong to this last dispensation. He speaks for God and claims that God did not show the Old Testament prophets the secret rapture, and so they were in ignorance (Sandeen, 65). Apparently, the New Testament authors and Jesus Himself are in this category. This slight-of-hand enabled Darby to pick and choose from both testaments what belonged to Israel and what to the church age. Darby believed that the Church age is so special that it caused Jesus to break the prophetic clock, and it would only be started up again after the secret rapture, when God would once again deal with the Jewish problem (Sandeen, 63).

Finally, the secret rapture is the source of the "any moment" teaching. By this he meant that Bible prophecy provides no milestones to help us discern how near we are to the second coming, and so it could be at any moment. His belief was that all of the biblical signs were only applicable to the time after his secret rapture. Then the prophetic clock would be restarted. Until then the church age is in complete ignorance until his secret rapture. This uninspired belief becomes the only sign for his followers. Jesus, on the other hand, gave his disciples signs to look for, (Matthew 24-25). Jesus was clear that the exact hour was unknowable, but He expected His disciples to be watching for it, (Matthew 24:36-44, Luke 12:35-40). Paul also was clear that He did not expect believers to be surprised or ignorant of the times (1 Thessalonians 5:1-11). Bible prophecy serves to help us see where we are in prophetic history. Darby's "any moment" teaching distorts this by making the claim that all of those prophetic milestones are to be thrown into the time of the last dispensation. Can you see why the fictional *Left Behind* series of books have so much material to work with.

Please note, Daniel 2 covers all of this history, from Daniel's day to the earth made new. I believe that Daniel is an inspired prophet. I am not so sure about Darby. If you look at Daniel 2, this metal man is a timeline that is absolutely unbroken. Not one break in time. Not one! All of the prophecies that we find in Daniel follow this pattern. In Daniel 7-9 and 10-12 God will come again to Daniel and expand upon the timeline we find in Chapter 2. God will fill-in historical periods that will reveal the rise of the papacy (Daniel 7), the great end-time judgment (Daniel 7-8), and God's entire dealings with Israel in Daniel 9, where the ministry of the Messiah is revealed.

Second, Darby is incorrect that the church goes up in a secret rapture while the sinners continue in some fictional last stand. In Matthew 13's famous parable of the wheat and the tares, Jesus specifically states that both sinner and saint grow together *until the very end*, the harvest, when the angel reapers bring in the wheat and bind the tares and burn them. It is amazing how one person could so satisfy the desires of the Jesuit counter reformation, leaving millions of Christians in the dark, while enabling an entire industry of fictional entertainment. More importantly, Darby becomes the founder of a new religion where he is its source of authority, its first pope. His secret rapture becomes the magic elixir that enables him to speak for God. God didn't reveal this. God wouldn't come back like that. God desired that the time prophecies should be broken.

Okay, now that we see Daniel for what he presents, let's return to the book of Daniel. Let's now discover how Daniel's message repeats and enlarges the history he has already revealed. In the process we will see how Daniel connects to Revelation. To do this I will not be using Darby as the lens through which I view the Bible. Instead, I will allow the Bible to speak for itself and let history be the guide to its fulfillment. This is clearly what is intended by Daniel 2, and it is found throughout Daniel. Does that sound fair. Let's get started.

READ DANIEL 7.

I know there are some strange images here, but get all the way through it and we can look at our next summary chart.

It is Daniel who has a dream and visions in this chapter. He sees a wind stirring up the Great Sea (Mediterranean Sea). Out of it come four beasts in consecutive order. The first a lion with wings. This would be easy for Daniel. He lived in Babylon where he would see this symbolism of a lion with wings displayed on the walls as he walks to the palace. Next comes this bear that is larger on one side than the other. The kingdoms of Media and Persia was just like this, with the Persians being much smaller. Its general Cyrus is the one who took out three nations, as depicted by the three ribs. Next, the incredibly fast leopard with four heads and four wings. Historically, Alexander the Great raced like a leopard in establishing the Greek kingdom. When he died young, his kingdom was divided by his strongest four generals. Finally, we arrive at the dreadful

Daniel 7 Summary Chart

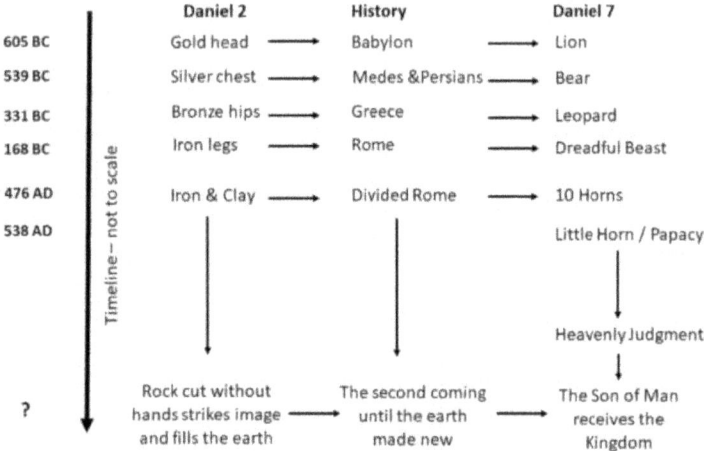

	Daniel 2	History	Daniel 7
605 BC	Gold head ⟶	Babylon ⟶	Lion
539 BC	Silver chest ⟶	Medes &Persians ⟶	Bear
331 BC	Bronze hips ⟶	Greece ⟶	Leopard
168 BC	Iron legs ⟶	Rome ⟶	Dreadful Beast
476 AD	Iron & Clay ⟶	Divided Rome ⟶	10 Horns
538 AD			Little Horn / Papacy
			↓
			Heavenly Judgment
			↓
?	Rock cut without hands strikes image ⟶ and fills the earth	The second coming until the earth ⟶ made new	The Son of Man receives the Kingdom

(Timeline– not to scale)

Figure 2.

beast with iron teeth that devoured. Iron was part of which kingdom in chapter two? That's right, its Rome. You can now understand how beasts in Bible prophecy can be used to represent kings, and kingdoms on the earth. You will find this throughout Daniel, and you will find this same thing happening in Revelation. Here at this point in Daniel 7 something about this Roman beast interested Daniel. It was the 10 horns on its head.

Can you see that Daniel 7 is tracking the same history as Daniel 2? Now, like Daniel, you can focus on the events within these time periods that are being enlarged with additional details. History records that the Roman kingdom really was different than the other three who were before it. Instead of being conquered like the others, Rome fell apart. The western Roman empire fell into 10 parts, and just like Daniel 2 tells us, there were attempts to put it back together through marriage and even conquest. The feet of iron and clay becomes a fitting description of the disintegration of the Roman Empire. History records that the split of the ten parts of the Western Roman Empire occurred around the year 476 AD.

During the interpretation, Daniel wants to know the truth about this period, and especially this little horn that arises among the ten divisions. We learn that this horn is different. It has a man at its head and it is boastful. It is fatter that the others and before it three horns were plucked up. As Daniel asks for this information, we find another interesting clue. Daniel describes the fourth beast's iron teeth and claws of bronze. When Rome conquered Greece it absorbed much of its culture, and progress. The common language throughout the Roman empire for commerce and learning was not Latin, but Greek. The New Testament was written in this common language.

Much of the interpretation deals with the little horn and provides us clues to identify this new power that arose upon the earth. First, the timing of its rise is after the 10 divisions of Rome were in place. This would be after 476 AD. Additionally, we find that three of the 10 were plucked up in its presence. When did that occur and who did it? Here is where you can see how the Book of Revelation helps us in interpreting what is happening now.

In Revelation chapter 13 the dragon of Revelation 12 is seen by a great sea and you watch as a singular beast rises out of it having seven heads and ten horns. It looks physically just like the dragon in chapter 12, except for several differences. First, are its body parts. As it arises out of the water you see them, leopard – bear – lion. Finally, you see all of it and notice the 10 horns with 10 crowns on them. This is none other than the Roman

Empire at the historical period where its ten divisions were in place. We notice something else. The dragon in chapter 12 has crowns on its seven heads, not on its horns. The head the devil was using in Chapter 12 was the kingdom of Rome which the devil used at the birth and death of the Messiah. Now the dragon is using this same head to pick a successor.

Historically, the capital of the Roman Empire during this period was Constantinople, located in modern Turkey. It was considered the Byzantine Empire at this time. Its Emperor Justinian was in the process of trying to regain control of some of the former western provinces that were troubling the Bishop of Rome. These were provinces dominated by Arians, considered Christian heretics. Justinian's campaign included the Heruli, Vandals, and the Ostrogoths. By 538 Rome was free of the control of the last of them. As the Revelation indicates, the Dragon gave this beast its power, seat, and great authority (Revelation 13:1-2). Thus, a new and different power arose on the world stage, and with it the beginning of the Holy Roman Empire. This is the little horn of Daniel 7.

The Holy Roman Empire, with its seat in Rome, truly was different from the others. It exerts its control through religion and dominates the rulers and peoples in this manner. The interpreters in Daniel 7 provide additional details that indicates that God's saints would be given into its hands for a specific prophetic period – a time, times, and half a time (Daniel 7:25). This famous time period in world history is found in both Daniel and Revelation. In Revelation 12 it is found as both a time, times, and half a time, and as 1260 days. We find it in Revelation 11 and 13 as 42 months. This is no accident. We are intended to see this period of days as prophetic years. It becomes an anchor to a period in world history and enables readers of

Daniel and the Revelation to know what period of history is highlighted[1]. This 1260 day/year period describes the undisputed reign of the papal Holy Roman Empire that ran from 538 to the year 1798 AD when it received a deadly wound during the French Revolution. See Figure 3.

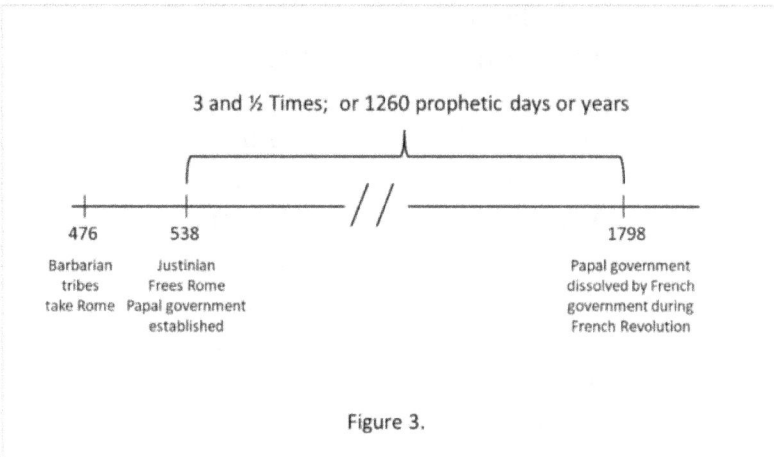

3 and ½ Times; or 1260 prophetic days or years

476	538	//	1798
Barbarian tribes take Rome	Justinian Frees Rome Papal government established		Papal government dissolved by French government during French Revolution

Figure 3.

It is this 1260-year period described in Daniel 7:25 that further highlights the characteristics of the little horn. During this period the papacy took upon itself the role of Christ on the earth. The pope became the vicar of the Son of God. In this boastful and prideful period it began to change the Christian religion into something completely

---

[1] This time prophecy is one of the most attested time prophecies in the entire Bible. This same period spanning 1260 years is described in Daniel 7:25 & Revelation 12:14 as a time and times and half a time (a time being one year – see Daniel 4:23). Revelation 12:6 talks about the same period describing this period as 1260 days, then later as three and a half times in verse 14. In Revelation 13:5 this time period is described as forty-two months. Taken together all of this points to 1260 literal years. (A day for a year – Consider Numbers 14:34 and Ezekiel 4:6 to find a biblical basis for interpreting these time prophecies.) It is amazing that in order to bolster his inventions, Darby specifically taught that these important time prophecies should be taken as days only. His followers are inconsistent in this, but the result is the same, distortion. Under Darby and Preterism the historicity of time prophecies in Daniel and Revelation are broken.

foreign to New Testament faith. It solidified a new priesthood, a new day of worship (Sunday), a new way to be saved, (the Mass, Penance, Indulgences), and new mediators between God and man the priests and the dead (Mary, and Relics).

To accomplish this, the papacy needed to change times and the law (verse 25). The Ten Commandments were altered so that people did not see the second commandment. It cut the tenth into two and shortened the fourth to hide its purpose in worship. It also murdered many of God's saints through its inquisitions. Only the Bible could bring light during these dark ages. It was the rediscovery of the Bible that led to the Protestant Reformation. It is said that millions were tortured and killed by this power. Truly the prophecy has revealed history in advance. In fact, the Bible commentators of the Protestant Reformation all saw the historicity and fulfillment of this 1260-year time prophecy as evidence that their historical approach to prophecy was sound.

Historian Ernest R. Sandeen provides a summary statement regarding the Protestant understanding of Bible prophecy at this time when he writes: *"The identification of the events of the 1790's with those prophesied in Daniel 7 and Revelation 13 provided biblical commentators with a prophetic Rosetta stone. At last, a key had been found with which to crack the code. There could now be general agreement upon one fixed point of correlation between prophecy and history"* (Sandeen, 7). The event in Revelation 13 that Sandeen references is the deadly wound of the sea beast of Revelation 13:3-4. Protestant reformers all recognized the Papacy as this sea beast in Revelation 13. As predicted in the prophecy, the Papacy received a deadly wound to its temporal power in 1798. The prophecy in Revelation 13:3 suggests that this deadly wound to one of the sea beast's heads will be miraculously resurrected to life again at a future point when the papacy would once again become a Church – State power. The final phase of this dramatic healing would see all the world wondering after this religious government and its pope.

Finally, we find that after this deadly wound, while the papacy is still in existence and still proudly boasting against heaven, a judgment scene is set up in heaven. This judgment happens prior to the Son of Man in Daniel 7:13-14 receiving the kingdom. During the interpretation it is revealed that at the conclusion of this end-time judgement the little horn would be consumed and destroyed forever (see Revelation 17). Then the saints would receive the kingdom set up by the Son of Man and it will fill the whole earth.

Did you notice that as the interpreter begins to tell the truth about the whole matter in Daniel 7, he first mirrors Daniel 2 before going on to give additional details regarding what is new in these periods. The angel interpreter simply says there would be four kingdoms and eventually the saints would win and receive the final kingdom set up by God (verses 17-18). This is important in understanding how to interpret Daniel. Daniel 2 must be seen as the guide. The history it provides is seen again and again, only having parts of these periods enlarged and expanded upon as we see here in Daniel 7. Keeping this in mind will help you avoid fanciful interpretations that are not derived from the text itself.

Second, can you see how time prophecy holds together the messages in Daniel and Revelation. These time prophecies, especially the 1260 year one, guide the reader to understand this incredible period in both Daniel and Revelation. The time prophecies serve to guide us historically and it is through them we find historical milestones, including the start of the pre-advent heavenly judgment described in Daniel 7. Distorting these time periods was a great triumph of the Jesuit counter reformation. The counter reformation tried hard to change how they are interpreted, and succeeded with Preterism by throwing them into the past, and Dispensational Futurism by denying their existence at all.

READ DANIEL 8.

Within three years of the vision of Daniel 7, Daniel receives another vision. In this vision the animals are familiar, a sheep and a goat. This goat is moving so fast its feet are not touching the ground. We don't need to guess what they represent. The angel interpreter of the vision plainly says the ram represents the kingdom of Media-Persia. The goat is the kingdom of Greece, and the horn on the goat we know is Alexander the Great. Are you seeing that Daniel 2, 7, and 8, are all speaking of the same historical periods. Here the vision begins with the silver kingdom in Daniel 2 and then transitions to the bronze, represented by the leopard in Daniel 7.

Next in history, the big horn of the goat is broken and four take its place. These we are told become kingdoms. We know historically that they were the kingdoms of Alexander's four strongest generals who divided it according to the four compass directions. Out of one of these will arises a new power called the little horn. This little horn is depicted has having two different intentions. The first is described as territorial. Coming from the north, it is seen devouring territory to the south east and the Glorious Land. This phase of the little horn describes the rise of what would become the Roman Empire.

Next the little horn is seen making an attempt at heaven itself. In this historical period of the little horn something is different. Its attack is vertical to God. It is seen as casting down things that belong in heaven and it even takes upon itself the authority of the Prince of the Host. This little horn is on the earth. It cannot actually bring the hosts of heaven down or be seen in heaven as replacing Jesus who is the only mediator between God and man. However, what the little horn is doing on the earth has the effect of accomplishing these things.

The little horn's actions on the earth cause the daily in heaven to lose its place. In the heavenly Sanctuary the daily represents the work of Jesus, our High Priest. It represents His mediation of atonement by His blood (read Hebrews 7-10). Now something dreadful has happened. The place that Christ holds in the Heavenly Sanctuary is now cast down to the earth. Shockingly, the little horn exalts itself to replace this important heavenly work with itself. This is a wanton criminal offence against heaven, and now we hear that "truth" is being cast to the ground in this period as earthly armies are given to the little horn to accomplish these things it is doing.

If you have been following Daniel 2-8, then you know that the little horn represents two periods of history. First the Roman Empire, and second, the Holy Roman Empire. The first is seen in the conquering of kingdoms on the earth, and the second in its conquering what only belongs in heaven during the 1260 years of the Holy Roman Empire. This period is so shocking to the holy ones in heaven that they are found to ask, how long is this going to go on? This criminal activity of the little horn in desolating what only belongs to Christ in heaven and trampling it under foot. An answer is given; "For two thousand three hundred days; then the sanctuary shall be cleansed" (Daniel 8:14).

A new mysterious time period is announced. A 2300 day/year time prophecy relating to an event that will begin when this 2300-year prophecy reaches its conclusion; the cleansing of the Sanctuary. In the interpretation Daniel is shown that its conclusion is near the end of the historical periods laid out in Daniel 2,7, and 8. It is called the time of the end, when a judgment in heaven will have commenced and the time for this little horn power to be destroyed, and Jesus is to take the kingdom. The key to understand this statement, "the sanctuary shall be cleansed" (KJV, and NKJV) is found in the imagery of this vision in Daniel 8.

Unlike the metal man of Daniel 2 or the crazy unreal beasts of Daniel 7, the beasts in Daniel 8 would be ones Daniel would have seen used in the earthly sanctuary in Jerusalem on a very special day. On the tenth day of the seventh month, God commanded Moses that a special service of atonement be made, known as the Day of Atonement, or Yom Kippur, which is a day of judgment and repentance for Israel. Only on this day, once a year, were both the ram (burnt offering) and the goat (scapegoat) used in the services of the Sanctuary. It was a day of judgment for Israel. Only on this day would the high priest enter into the most holy place of the Sanctuary. Starting there, he would cleanse the mercy seat with blood, then the altar of incense, thereby removing the sins stored in the Tabernacle, sins that were atoned for by the blood of the sacrifices during the year. Now, the responsibility for those sins is placed upon the head of the scapegoat and it is removed from the presence of Israel. This is the imagery Daniel was shown to describe an event that will happen in heaven at the conclusion of the 2300 days/years of this prophecy. The same event that is depicted in Daniel 7 as the heavenly judgment that occurs prior to the Son of Man receiving the kingdom. We can now make the connection between Daniel 8 and what we have seen earlier in Daniel. See Figure 4.

I hope that the symmetry, and purpose of these revelations to Daniel impresses you. It is amazing that all of this history has been told in advance. It reveals the heart of the dragon's war to overthrow the ministry of the Messiah (compare Revelation 13). It shows historically where and from what world kingdom this indignation would arise. It uncovers the blasphemy of the plan the devil conjures up to receive worship from an earthly religion, one that proudly claims to be the replacement on earth for the Messiah. It also connects us with the final gospel cry of God's remnant in Revelation 14, who pronounce that the hour of judgment has come for the people on the earth. Now, all that remains is to find the end date of this 2300 days/years prophecy to reveal the beginning of a final end-time judgment that precedes the end of this indignation and the coming of the Son of Man.

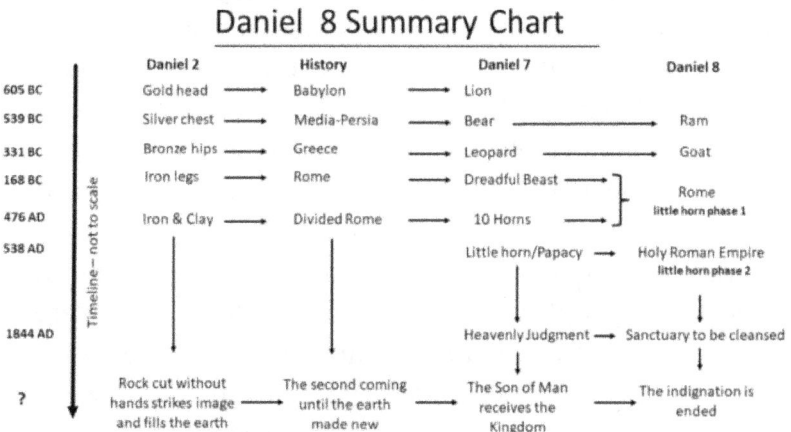

Daniel 8 Summary Chart

		Daniel 2		History		Daniel 7		Daniel 8
605 BC		Gold head	→	Babylon	→	Lion		
539 BC		Silver chest	→	Media-Persia	→	Bear	→	Ram
331 BC		Bronze hips	→	Greece	→	Leopard	→	Goat
168 BC	Timeline – not to scale	Iron legs	→	Rome	→	Dreadful Beast → ⎤		Rome
476 AD		Iron & Clay	→	Divided Rome	→	10 Horns → ⎦		little horn phase 1
538 AD						Little horn/Papacy →		Holy Roman Empire little horn phase 2
1844 AD						Heavenly Judgment →		Sanctuary to be cleansed ↓
?		Rock cut without hands strikes image and fills the earth	→	The second coming until the earth made new	→	The Son of Man receives the Kingdom	→	The indignation is ended

Figure 4.

READ DANIEL 9

Daniel did not understand the meaning of this long 2300 day/year period that he was shown in Daniel 8. This becomes clearer when he begins seeking forgiveness for his sins and the sins of Israel in the past. Daniel was certain that Jeremiah's prophecy of the return of his people to the land of Israel was at hand. How does this incredible puzzle of the 2300 years before the sanctuary is cleansed fit into any of that? Daniel specifically prays on behalf of the people and the desolated city of Jerusalem and God's desolated sanctuary there. While he is still praying the angel Gabriel, whom he saw earlier in Daniel 8, comes again to give Daniel understanding of the part of the vision in chapter 8 that was still not understood. In the process, Gabriel reveals God's total and final dealings with Old Covenant Israel.

Daniel is told that a time period from heaven has been imposed upon Daniel's people, Old Covenant Israel. Seventy weeks, or 70 times 7 days per week, to give 490 days or prophetic years. It would make no sense at all if this period was a literal 490 days. Nothing Gabriel says next would match with anything in history if this period of days were not literal prophetic years. During this period several things will take place. First, God deals with the sin problem and reconciles it. Righteousness will be revealed that is unending. Old Testament vision and prophecy will meet its conclusion, as the Most Holy is anointed (Daniel 9:24). Clearly, all of this points to the Messiah, Jesus Christ. A reading of the Gospels in the New Testament will reveal that people both inside and outside of Israel were expecting the Messiah to come at any moment. Jesus was the fulfillment of this prophecy, since His death on the cross dealt with the sin problem and reconciled God with sinners. Jesus brought in everlasting righteousness. This would be His righteousness, that sinners receive when they believe. The prophecies of the Old Testament point to the work of the Messiah both as the sin bearing Savior (Isaiah 53) and a conquering King, (Psalms 2:9). Daniel is now shown the first period of the Messiahs work as a sin bearing Savior.

Next, Gabriel gives the starting point for the 2300 days/years prophecy of Daniel 8, by which the seventy weeks is determined (literally, "cut off"). Remember, Gabriel came to give Daniel understanding of what was not explained or understood completely in Daniel 8. Cut off from this larger 2300-year prophecy is a 490-year period that deals with Israel. Daniel is now told the starting point of them both. This starting point is the decree that will result in the restoration, and rebuilding of Jerusalem. That is good news for humanity. Of the several decrees that enabled the Jews to return back to Israel, and rebuild the temple the third one provided authorization and funds to restore the city itself. The specific one is even recorded in the book of Ezra chapter seven. The decree of Artaxerxes in 457 BC, gave the Jews political authority, and finances to complete the city. Ezra 7:8 gives the clue to finding this starting point. It was in the seventh year of the king Artaxerxes. Fortunately for us the dates for the reign of Artaxerxes are well known. Archaeological discoveries have helped to refine the many ancient sources that tracked the reigns of certain rulers in the ancient near east. From these it was determined that the seventh year was 457 BC, as recorded by the Jewish civil calendar (Shea, 64-66).

Next, from this starting point of 457 BC Gabriel now announces that after 69 of those weeks the Messiah the Prince would arrive! Four hundred and eighty-three years and the prophesied Messiah would come. This 483-year period is divided into two sections, a smaller section of 49 years (7 weeks) and a larger one consisting of 434 years (62 weeks). It is again pointed out that the rebuilding of Jerusalem is the activity that would occur sometime in the

483-year period. Does the Gospel's help us determine if Daniel's prophecy is accurate? When did the Messiah arrive?

The event that we are looking for is the baptism of Jesus. The word Messiah, or Christ, means "anointed one." At Jesus' baptism it was clearly seen by John the Baptist, that Jesus was anointed by the Holy Spirit and announced by the Father. The three synoptic gospels, Matthew, Mark and Luke, contain the actual event (for example Matthew 3). The gospel of John records the motivation for why John the Baptist was baptizing in the first place.

> 33 I did not know Him, but He who sent me to baptize with water said to me, 'Upon whom you see the Spirit descending, and remaining on Him, this is He who baptizes with the Holy Spirit.' 34 And I have seen and testified that this is the Son of God" (John 1:33–34, NKJV).

To determine the timing of this event we will need the names of historical figures and events that took place in their lives to fix a year that this event took place. Fortunately, Luke 3 provides such an account. We learn that the year Jesus was baptized was in the fifteenth year of the reign of Tiberius Caesar, when Pontius Pilate was governor of Judea, Herod was tetrarch of Galilee, his brother Philip was tetrarch of the region of Ituraea and Trachonitis, and Lysanias was tetrarch of Abilene, in the high priesthood of Annas, and Caiaphas (Luke 3:1). Whew! This amazing list provides historians the exact year the baptism took place. Tiberius Caesar actually began his reign over Judea as a prince. In 12 A.D. Tiberius began his coregency with this father Augustus Caesar. Adding 15 years to 12 A.D. and we arrive at the year 27 A.D. for the baptism of Jesus. Amazingly, the Messiah came right on time! Please see Figure 5.

Daniel 9 Summary

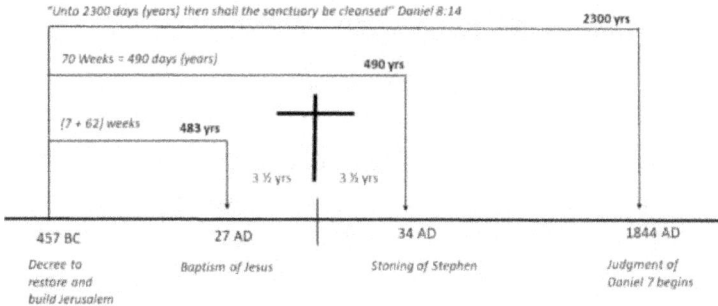

Figure 5.

When you try to check these dates, remember that the dating system has no year zero like a number line does. Your calculation might look like this 467-483=26. You will need to add one since your calculator also subtracted zero in the calculation.

As you can see in Figure 5, there is a bit more to the prophecy of the Messiah and the city Jerusalem left to study. Verses 26-27 provides additional information on the fate of the Messiah and the fate of Jerusalem. First, we learn that after His anointing the Messiah will be killed. This death is not for Himself but for the people. Verse 27 gives us the timing of when this will take place. It states that He, the Messiah, will confirm a covenant with the people for one week (7 days/years). In the middle of that week (3.5 years) the Messiah will bring an end to the temple sacrificial system with its offerings. The sacrificial system, or law of Moses, would be found in the document that was hung on the outside of the Ark of the Covenant (Deuteronomy 31:24-26). This Book of the Law contained the ceremonial laws, including the services of the Sanctuary and the blessings and curses, and was specifically there as a witness against the people. In the middle of the week, Jesus our Savior ended that system by his death on the cross (See Colossians 2:14; Ephesians 2:14-15). It is absolutely amazing how the prophecy is so accurately fulfilled in Jesus Christ.

Three and a half years after the cross, the end of God's dealings with Old Covenant Israel is completed. The event that marks this ending is the year of Stephen's testimony to the people and trial before the Jewish religious leaders (Acts 6-7). Stephen's testimony to them was rejected and he was brutally stoned to death. That day a great persecution of the church in Jerusalem took place and they were scattered and began preaching the word in Gentile areas. That day a man named Saul of Tarsus was present. Saul sought permission to go after the Christians in Damascus and on his journey, he met the resurrected Jesus. Saul (later Paul) would become the great missionary evangelist and church planter. Through his writings we can trace back to the year of his conversion, the year Stephen was killed.

In the book of Galatians Paul recollects his beginnings as a Christian and gives a biography of important events, specifically times he visited Jerusalem, three years after his conversion and a second time fourteen years later. The second visit is recorded in Acts 15. That year Paul began his second missionary journey, which ended up in Corinth (Acts 18). While there he wound up before a proconsul named Gallio. History records that Gallio's one-year proconsul in Corinth was in the year 51 AD. Going back seventeen years would place the stoning of Stephen, the rejection of Christ by the Jewish leaders, the scattering of Christians, and the conversion of Saul to be the year 34 AD. Amazingly, this year also agrees with the ending of the

490-year prophecy concerning Old Covenant Israel (Shea, 68-69).

Now our chart in Figure 5 is complete with the activities of Messiah the Prince and the ending of the 2300-year prophecy in 1844 AD. Both of these events are described by the prophet Daniel and both point us to our great hope. First, the salvation that we have in Jesus the Messiah and second, the beginning of the final judgment, that becomes for us a milestone that helps us see the day in which we are living. With the fulfilment of this longest time prophecy, the earth is entering into the time of the end mentioned by Gabriel to Daniel in chapter 8. Lift up your heads, for your redemption is near.

Before we leave Daniel 9, there are still parts of verses 26 and 27 that have not been discussed. Remember, one of Daniel's big concerns was with the city Jerusalem. Throughout Gabriel's explanations to Daniel, the city was in the forefront. With the killing of the Messiah, something is predicted to happen to the city as well. Verse 26 indicates that in the future, a prince would bring his army and destroy the city and its sanctuary. Its destruction would happen rapidly, and it would be seen as an abomination of desolation, which would one day be paid back on the desolator (verse 27).

The destruction of Jerusalem in 70 AD is a historical event that Jesus also predicted. In Luke 21 we hear Jesus say:

> [20] "But when you see Jerusalem surrounded by armies, then know that its desolation is near. [21] Then let those who are in Judea flee to the mountains, let those who are in the midst of her depart, and let not those who are in the country enter her. [22] For these are the days of vengeance,

that all things which are written may be fulfilled (Luke 21:20–22, NKJV).

The "things that are written" that must be fulfilled is the prophecy of the desolation of Jerusalem in Daniel 9. Just as it was predicted, a prince, named Titus brought the armies of Rome to Jerusalem and completely desolated it, looted it, burned it, and did not leave one stone upon another.

Figure 6 provides an aid to better understand the events in Daniel 9:24-27. J. B. Doukhan reveals in his book on Daniel that there is an intentional chiastic structure to Daniel 9:25-27 (Doukhan, 146). Realizing this provides a methodology in unpacking this amazing prophecy. In Figure 6, I have ordered the chiastic pairs in a chart that highlights the important focus of Gabriel's message. Notice how the emphasis is on what happens to the Messiah and then to the city.

Focus of Gabriel's message to Daniel

The Messiah	The City
Coming of Messiah	Rebuilding of city /temple
Messiah Cut Off	City to be Cut Off
Messiah's Covenant Ends the sacrificial system	City / temple comes to an end

Figure 6.

I realize that if your background is either Preterist or if you are a disciple of Darby, this may be the first time you have seen prophecy like this. As a Preterist you have been taught to deny it all. As a Dispensational Futurist you have also been deceived. It is this very 490-year prophecy in Daniel 9 that Darby monkeyed with. Using the magic of his invention, the secret rapture, Darby himself cuts this prophecy and throws part of the last week into the distant future. All of this to create his last dispensation, where God will supposedly deal with Old Covenant Israel again! What truly belongs to the Messiah the disciples of Darby give to the Antichrist. Using Darby's theories, these modern-day fiction writers have completely masked and distorted the beauty and symmetry of Daniel's prophecy and its connection to the Revelation. Darby launched what would turn out to be a new religion. Millions of Christians locked into one of Darby's dispensations are being taught to ignore the central role of sola scriptura, allowing all of scripture be a guide in interpreting itself. Many Christians are ignorant of the New Covenant and the fact that Israel today is the Christian Church (Romans 11; Revelation 12). As a result of the counter reformation Jesuits, today's Christians are left behind. They are blind to what prophecy actually depicts, and we see Protestants being drawn back to the Roman Catholic Church. Protestants will have a large role in leading the world to worship an image to the sea beast and to take its mark and number. By joining themselves back to Rome they will unwittingly get on the wrong ride at the end. The Jesuit creators of these counter reformation falsehoods could only imagine how successful their works would be.

Chapter 3

The Second Coming
What does the Bible say?

In the thirteenth chapter of the Gospel of John, Jesus begins to announce to His disciples that he is leaving them to go to a place they cannot follow. In Christ's final moments alone with His disciples Jesus leaves them with a promise.

> 1 Let not your heart be troubled: ye believe in God, believe also in me. 2 In my Father's house are many mansions: if *it were* not *so*, I would have told you. I go to prepare a place for you. 3 And if I go and prepare a place for you, I will come again, and receive you unto myself; that where I am, *there* ye may be also (John 14:1–3 KJV).

This simple promise of going away and then returning once again now forms the basis of the Christian hope. This promise of coming again creates a living hope, one that is undefiled and will not fade, reserved in heaven, and kept by God through faith for salvation that will be revealed at the end when this promise is realized (1 Peter 1:3-5). The time of Jesus return now becomes known as the second time for the appearance of Jesus, or simply as the second coming. For example, consider:

> 28 So Christ was once offered to bear the sins of many; and unto them that look for him shall he appear the second time without sin unto salvation (Hebrews 9:28, KJV).

I want you to consider the importance the Bible places on the second coming being the actual appearance of Jesus. The form of this Greek verb in Hebrews 9:28 implies that the appearance is visible. It will be something that you see and not figurative. Jesus will appear, and it will be the second time or the second literal, physical, coming, when the plan of salvation will become complete for the faithful.

After the resurrection of Jesus, the Lord met with his disciples one last time to commission them and share the promise of the Holy Spirit. It is recorded that after this the disciples visibly saw Jesus rising in the air until He went into a cloud and they could no longer see Him. Immediately after this event two heavenly messengers stand next to the disciples and declare that Jesus would return just like that (Acts 1:9-11). These messengers are only repeating what Jesus told his disciples earlier, that the sign of his appearing would be the sight of Him coming on the clouds of heaven with great power and glory (Matthew 24:27-31; Mark 13:24-27). Even the religious leaders in Jerusalem, who condemned Jesus for admitting that He is the Messiah, are told by Jesus that they will be resurrected to witness this sign, and see the Lord sitting in power, and coming on the clouds (Matthew 26:64; Mark 14:62). Paul remarks that on this day the saints still living and the resurrected dead *"will be caught up together in the clouds, to meet the Lord in the air"* (1 Thessalonians 4:15-18). The final New Testament witness of this event is found in the first chapter of Revelation, where it reads:

> 7 Behold, he cometh with clouds; and every eye shall see him, and they *also* which pierced him: and all kindreds of the earth shall wail because of him. Even so, Amen (Revelation 1:7, KJV).

If you take the time to read all the texts that I have just shared, you will soon come to the conclusion that the second coming is a literal, visible, unmistakable, loud, and incredible sign that becomes the realization of the salvation brought to the saints through Jesus Christ, our Lord and Savior. It is the realization of the promise Jesus gave to His disciples and also to the religious leaders who condemned Him. His coming on that day also brings destruction to the wicked, (Zephaniah 1:14-18; Revelation 6:12-17; Revelation 14).

With all that the Bible says about the second coming of Jesus, it is sad that over time deception would creep in and change the plain meaning of the text. This happened during the life of Paul. We read in his second letter to the Thessalonian church that some people were troubling the church, writing in Paul's name, and making a claim that the second coming has already occurred. Paul reassures the believers that this is impossible, since as he has already shared with them, the second coming cannot occur until there is an apostasy that comes from within the church itself. It is an apostasy that reveals a Christian power that exalts itself, pretends to take the place of God, and desires the worship that only God deserves. This power would work in league with Satan and will deceive many people in this way (2 Thessalonians 2:1-12). This has to happen before the second coming. Can you see how the prophecies of Daniel and Revelation help us to discover the milestones in history when that apostate Christian power would rise.

Friends, prophecy has more to tell. The purpose of this work is to move us past what I have already shown you and to look at what prophecy says will happen on the earth right before the second coming. We will look at some additional milestones in prophecy that help us understand how near we really are, what movements in the world proceed it, and how to prepare for it. Are you ready? Let's begin by looking at an important sign of the end.

CHAPTER 4

The Sign of the End - Part 1

The Message of the Mighty Angel

There is a message from the Sanctuary in heaven that comes to humanity for our times. The message is found in Revelation 10:1-7 and concerns people living today. In Revelation 10:1 we find a mighty angel coming down from heaven. This angel comes with the authority of God. The angel is seen as coming in the clouds, a rainbow on his head, his face shining like the face of Moses when he was in the presence of God. His similar appearance to Christ in Revelation 1, indicates that the message comes from our Lord Jesus Christ. The visuals continue as we see a little scroll that was open in the angel's hands, his feet standing on the earth and sea. This message is not limited to a geographic area, but is for the whole world.

Then comes the climactic moment when the angel cries out in a lion-like roar and seven thunders speak words that are not to be written. The lion roar and the voice of thunder are both signs that this message comes directly from God (See Hosea 11:10; John 12:28-30). The purpose of the lion roar and thundering voice is to impress on the remnant the importance of what the angel says, and the need to listen to the message that follows. The message is an oath that comes directly from God.

> *5 And the angel which I saw stand upon the sea and upon the earth lifted up his hand to heaven, 6 And sware by him that liveth for ever and ever, who created heaven, and the things that therein are, and*

*the earth, and the things that therein are, and the
sea, and the things which are therein, that there
should be time no longer: 7 But in the days of the
voice of the seventh angel, when he shall begin to
sound, the mystery of God should be finished, as he
hath declared to his servants the prophets* (Revelation
10:5–7, KJV).

The purpose of this important oath is twofold: first to
announce an end of prophetic time, and second, an end of
gospel time. This is not a single point in time, but rather a
season of time that occurs between two points. This
season begins and ends during the events under the sixth
Trumpet. It identifies the starting and ending points of the
final season of grace for humanity before the end comes.

Let's start with the proclamation that time will no
longer be. The word in the original language is the Greek
word *chronos*, from which we get the word chronometer.
It implies a measurement of time. We cannot assume that
what ends is time itself. In the oath, historical events
continue to take place after this point and ultimately take
us to the sounding of the seventh trumpet, which heralds
the return of Christ.[2] So, it is not talking about time itself,
but rather something that is measured in time. What is
implied by this statement is the *end of prophetic time*. The
time measurements that are found in the books of Daniel
and Revelation will have reached their conclusion, their
end points. The oath implies that we will not find any
other prophecies based upon time after this point. So,
when will that be?

---

[2] In this book I am referring to a premillennial Second Coming of the Lord
that is loud, unmistakable, and results in the resurrection of the saints and
the destruction of the wicked.

When you look at the time prophecies of Daniel, the longest of them is the 2300 days/years prophecy of Daniel 8:14, which reached its conclusion in the year 1844. This statement in the angel's oath now becomes for us a starting point for a season of time that will ultimately end with the seventh trumpet blast. This means that for us living today there is no delay. There is nothing holding back the final events. Humanity is living at the time of the end, and the fulfillment of this longest time prophecy now marks the beginning of this final season before the seventh trumpet blast and the second coming of our Lord. Now, let's look at the rest of this oath and discover what it implies for God's people laboring for Jesus at the end.

While the first part of the oath declares the end of prophetic time, the second half of the oath now announces the end of *gospel time*. The oath declares that when the seventh angel trumpet blast is just about to sound the mystery of God will be finished. What is the "mystery of God?" According to apostle Paul, the mystery of God is the gospel concerning Jesus Christ. Paul says that it was kept secret since the world began, but now is made manifest by the prophetic word found in the Scriptures (Romans 16:25-26; Colossians 1:24-27; Ephesians 3:8-9). In his letter to the Ephesian church, Paul declares that the mystery was revealed to him by revelation and declares that its subject is the gospel of Christ (Ephesians 3:1-6). To the Colossian church Paul equates the mystery with New Covenant gospel faith revealed by the indwelling of Christ in the hearts of the believers (Colossians 1:27). With Paul's prophetic witness, it is safe to conclude that the "mystery" in the angel's oath is the gospel of Jesus Christ our Lord. So, what does it mean when the angel says that it is finished?

The exact word that is found in the original language is the ancient Greek word *teleo*. The basic meaning of this word is to bring some activity to a close (BDAG). To finish it. What is not implied in this text is that the purpose of the activity is complete, or has been completed. By using the aorist passive form of the verb, the implication is that something, or someone brought the activity to a close. The context of the passage is the mystery of God, and the activity of closing it is further highlighted by the fact that God already spoke of this closing activity to his prophets. This evidence leads to the conclusion that this is a "divine passive." During a space of time right before the sounding of the seventh trumpet, God will close this activity. God will end gospel time. Many have called this action the close of probation; a period of time immediately before the return of Christ where God closes access to the mediation of Christ's atonement.

An illustration of this closing of probation is visually depicted in Revelation 15. This chapter begins with the introduction of the seven angels who have the seven last plagues. The purpose of the plagues being described with the phrase; "for in them the wrath of God is complete" (Revelation 15:1). The word "complete" is again the Greek word *teleo*, having the same aorist passive form as seen in Revelation 10:7 that we just studied. In the context it is again a divine passive. It points to the fact that the plagues represent actions that bring to a conclusion the wrath of God. You could think of them as sitting in a rollercoaster. In most rollercoasters there is a period of delay as the cars rise slowly up a steep hill. Now imagine you have reached the very top and you know that once you go over the top the ride will not stop until it gets to the end. In the same way, these seven plagues result in world events that will not conclude until the world reaches the end with the second coming of the Lord Jesus Christ.

As you look further into Revelation 15, you find the next scene is a peak into the future. God's people who went through the last events are once again seen standing before the throne of God. The last time you saw the redeemed was in Revelation 7:9-17. They are described there as a great multitude, who washed their robes in the blood of the Lamb. Here there is an additional mention of the fact that they were victorious over the beast, over his image, over his mark, and over the number of his name. They sing a song from two experiences, that of Moses and that of the Lamb. We hear that song, and then we are brought back to the events associated with the seven angels with the seven last plagues.

Now in Revelation 15:5, we are brought to the temple of God in heaven. It is described with the same language as found in the book of Exodus for the Sanctuary. This makes sense since Moses was instructed in its design based upon the Sanctuary that is in heaven (Hebrews 8:4-5). It is called the "tabernacle of the testimony in heaven." This should bring pause to Christians who have been taught that the "testimony," the Ten Commandments, have been done away with. Not here! It is clear from this imagery that the basis of the New Covenant is the same as in the Old Covenant – The testimony of God, the Ten Commandments (Hebrews 8:7-13). Next, we see the temple filled with smoke from both the glory of God and His power. Then we hear the message that probation had closed for humanity "and no one was able to enter the temple till the seven plagues of the seven angels were completed" (Revelation 15:8). There will be no access to the place where Jesus our High Priest has been mediating the atonement in His blood. The world has reached the peak of the last ride. The end is coming.

Those who have studied Bible prophecy have noticed that the imagery we see in Revelation 15 has been seen before. It is found in the book of the prophet Ezekiel. In chapters 8 – 10 Ezekiel is witness to the apostasy of God's people. He witnesses a judgment scene where a figure having a writing device is marking the people, "who sigh and cry over all the abominations that are done within it" (Ezekiel 9:4). The hour of judgment has been completed and now the command is given to pour out wrath on the apostate religion.[3] The last scenes in Ezekiel graphically depict the closing of probation for Israel as a cloud fills the temple from the glory of the Lord so that no man could enter it. God is depicted as departing. I can't think of a greater illustration of what is being described both in the oath from heaven in Revelation 10 and in Revelation 15, just prior to the seven last plagues pouring out on the earth.

SUMMARY

At this point I would like to summarize what we have learned from the oath found in Revelation 10. First, the oath points us to a time just prior to the blowing of the seventh trumpet, heralding the return of Christ (Revelation 11:15-18). The oath depicts a period in time with specific start and end points (See Figure 7).

---

[3] We find something similar happening at the end where apostate religion is depicted as Babylon the Great. The final plagues that fall on the earth are specifically for the apostate Christianity that exists at the end. (See Revelation 18:4)

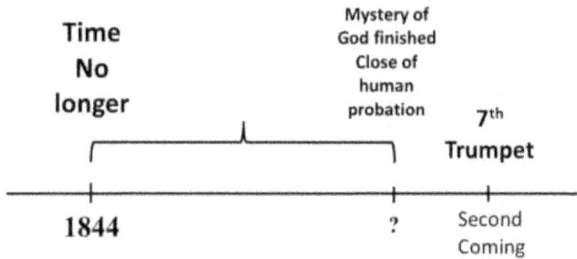

Figure 7.

The starting point is the decree that prophetic time is no more. This is the sign that a last season of grace remains. It is a time that ends with God closing the mystery of the gospel of Christ just prior to the sounding of the seventh trumpet blast. So, where are we in all of this? The events of Revelation 10-11, are all part of the period of time that falls under the sixth trumpet. The entire world is living in this span of time which began with the end of prophetic time and runs to the close of human probation. How near are we to this important event?

Chapter 5

The Sign of the End – Part 2

THE POWER OF GOD'S PEOPLE IS GONE

If you have ever read the book of the prophet Daniel, then you know that God revealed world events that span thousands of years. The prophecy of the metal man in Daniel 2 reveals a span of time that starts around 605 B.C. and runs until the events of Revelation 21-22 have taken place; from Daniel's day to the earth made new. It is an incredible prophecy that also depicts world events in symbolic imagery. There are two other places where an expansion and enlargement of this same time frame is given. However, this time with specific historical periods enlarged to give the reader important information. You find this in both Daniel 7-9 and in Daniel 10-12. Each of these sections highlights important way points in prophetic history. However, the important point to make is that the history presented in all of them is within the overall period of time covered by Daniel 2.

With this introduction, I would like us to focus on the last major prophetic section, Daniel 10-12, and specifically the events that occur in chapter 12. The last chapter in the prophecy of Daniel is a summary of last events. It begins with the announcement of an event in heaven that results in the final time of trouble for the people of the earth. This earth-shaking tribulation is followed by the rescue of God's people at the second coming of Christ. Let's look at this together.

¹ And at that time shall Michael stand up, the great prince which standeth for the children of thy people: and there shall be a time of trouble, such as never was since there was a nation *even* to that same time: and at that time thy people shall be delivered, every one that shall be found written in the book. ² And many of them that sleep in the dust of the earth shall awake, some to everlasting life, and some to shame *and* everlasting contempt. ³ And they that be wise shall shine as the brightness of the firmament; and they that turn many to righteousness as the stars for ever and ever (Daniel 12:1–3, KJV).

The standing up of Michael results in the last day events described here as a time of trouble that will be greater than any before it. This is good news for God's people because at that time they will be delivered. The history we are seeing spans the period from the closing of the mystery of God to the white throne judgment of Revelation 20 and the earth made new. We see two resurrections; the resurrection of life and the resurrection of damnation, spoken by our Lord Jesus Christ (John 5:29). Following this is a picture of the saints shining as stars for ever and ever.

Next, we hear that Daniel is to seal up the words of his book. These last events are not for his day. We are told the book is to be sealed until the time of the end. As time progresses knowledge will increase and at the end this book will be completely open. Heaven declares that at the end, this open book must be shared again with the people of the earth (Revelation 10:8-11). At the end it will speak.

Suddenly, in chapter 12, we see the heavenly being who first came to Daniel at the Tigris River to give him understanding (Daniel 10). The description of this being is very similar to both Jesus in Revelation's first chapter and the mighty angel in Revelation 10. A question is asked, and once again we watch a heavenly being make an important oath from God.

> 5 Then I Daniel looked, and, behold, there stood other two, the one on this side of the bank of the river, and the other on that side of the bank of the river. 6 And one said to the man clothed in linen, which was upon the waters of the river, How long shall it be to the end of these wonders? 7 And I heard the man clothed in linen, which was upon the waters of the river, when he held up his right hand and his left hand unto heaven, and sware by him that liveth for ever that it shall be for a time, times, and an half; and when he shall have accomplished to scatter the power of the holy people, all these things shall be finished (Daniel 12:5–7, KJV).

The oath contains a question. When will everything that God showed Daniel finally be fulfilled? When will the end of all these wonders come about? The answer reveals a period of time whose beginning and ending are identified by two events. The first event is the conclusion of a time prophecy. The prophecy in question is found in Daniel 7. It is related to a religious and political power that arises out of the breakup of the western Roman Empire. During this 1260-year period God's people will be directly under the control of the little horn (Daniel 7:25). Protestant reformers have identified this three-and-a-half times, or 1260 day/year period, as the rise of the papacy in 538 A.D. until it received a deadly wound in 1798, when Napoleon ended its temporal power[4]. Since this prophetic time

---

[4] This prophetic time period is mentioned in Daniel and in Revelation. In Revelation 12 it is described as 1260 days, and also as a time, times and a half (Revelation 12:6; 14). These time periods are related to the Christian

period is past, the first condition has been met, but what about the second?

The second condition that acts as the end point to the heavenly being's oath refers specifically to the condition of God's people when the end comes. The text indicates that all the wonders in Daniel's prophecy conclude *when the influence of God's holy people is finally extinguished.* Think of God's holy people as a fire that brings light into this dark world. This prophecy indicates that there will come a time when the influence of that light will be diminished, and only the coals of the fire remain. Have you ever seen a campfire where the flame finally goes out? Before this, the flame has influence to bring light to push back the darkness. Even a small flame gives needed light. When the flame dies out, only the hot coals remain, but their light is no match for the darkness.

In the Hebrew language there are two verbs that describe the action that is causing the influence of God's holy people to diminish to nothing. The first of these verbs is typically used to describe something that is shattered, broken, or even pulverized (Psalms 2:9; Isaiah 27:9; Jeremiah 51:21-23). The object of this shattering action in Daniel 12:7 is the influence, (power) of God's holy people at the end. The reason I used the English word "influence" is that the Hebrew word translated here as "power" literally is a person's arm or forearm. It talks about a person's ability to do something. It talks about their ability to control or influence the outcome of an activity. In Daniel 12:7 we find that the end comes when the influence

---

church and span 1260 years. During the rise of the papacy from 538 A.D. – 1798 A.D. Christians were persecuted by this power. The papacy has attempted to change God's law. In Revelation 13:5 this same time period is called 42 months, and describes similar activities.

of God's holy people is shattered. Whatever influence or
ability they had in the past is now completely gone.

The reason it is gone is found in the second verb which
describes an action that continues until it has reached its
goal. Picture in your mind a pretty clay figurine. Now
watch as a person picks up a hammer, and repeatedly hits
the figurine until it's now unrecognizable. It's just a bunch
of broken clay dust on the table. That is the idea. The oath
declares that before Daniel's wonders end, forces will
finally, and completely, shatter the influence of God's holy
people. I say this because in the construct of these two
verbs, it is the influence of God's people, not God's people
themselves, that is the direct object of the action of these
verbs. For example, if I say "Jeff walks the dog," the direct
object (dog) is put in motion by the action of Jeff. In the
case of God's holy people, the direct object of the
shattering is their influence. At the end the power of God's
holy people will be gone. At the end there will come
movements whose end goal is to box in and eliminate the
influence of Bible believing Christians.

The reason that I qualify here that it is the influence of
Bible believing Christians being shattered is the fact that
prophecy indicates that at the end of time apostate religion
will prosper. Revelation 17 describes visually this
apostate religion as Babylon the Great, the mother of
harlots. At the very end this apostate religious power
briefly sits upon secular world governments. If you study
the apostacy of ancient Israel and Judah, one of the
complaints from God is their lusting after the governments
of other nations, and their desire for them. The lament
over Babylon's destruction comes from the nations she
prostituted herself with. The warning to God's people is to
come out of her so that you do not receive her plagues.

If you are a Bible believing Christian living today, you need to ask yourself if there are forces that are attempting to silence your voice and your influence? How safe do you feel to speak your beliefs at your job, or in your public school or university. Are you able to speak outside of your church group about issues related to the rampant sexual immorality and practices that are condemned in the Bible? At the time I write this, people are being arrested for silent prayer in certain places. The hostility of governments towards biblical faith and practice is growing, and prophecy indicates that one day it will reach a point where its light will be extinguished.

SUMMARY

This extinguishing of the light of God's holy people becomes the sign that the end is near. When the light is put out, Michael stands up, and the mystery of God is finished. It becomes the sign of the end. God does not want His people living at the end to wonder what is happening to them. So, God sends these sworn oaths from His heavenly throne to warn the believers so they will not lose hope. In Revelation 10 the oath reveals the end of gospel time. In Daniel 12 the oath answers the questions of when will all these wonders be fulfilled. The answer is when the influence of God's true people is finally extinguished. The light that it brought to the world is gone. The coals (the remnant people of God) are still there, but are helpless to restart the flame. This is the sign of the end (See Figure 8).

The sign of the end

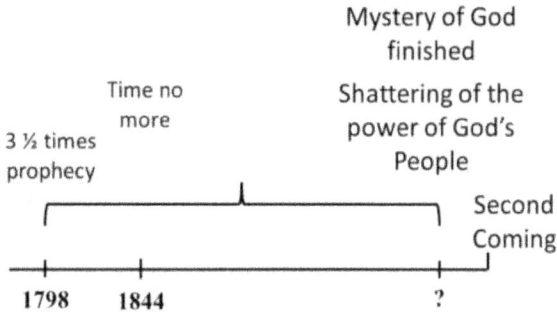

Figure 8.

If you are a Bible believing Christian take heart. With the closing of the sixth angel's trumpet comes the sounding of the seventh. Let's look at it together.

> 15 Then the seventh angel sounded: And there were loud voices in heaven, saying, "The kingdoms of this world have become *the kingdoms* of our Lord and of His Christ, and He shall reign forever and ever!" (Revelation 11:15, NKJV).

While it looks as if all is lost, nothing was really out of God's control. In fact, as we move into what the Bible says about Armageddon you will find that all of this was part of the plan.

Chapter 6

Armageddon

With the mystery of God being finished and Michael standing up, the world will experience what the Bible calls the seven last plagues. If you study these plagues in Revelation 16 you will find that they have a pattern to them. They are antitypes of events that you find in the Old Testament. This tells us that to gain a better understanding of the events, it would be helpful to go back and look at the types found in the history of Israel.

The first type we find in the seven last plagues is what is called the Exodus from Egypt typology. In the book of Exodus God desired to free his people enslaved in Egypt. The problem was Pharaoh was not going to allow this to happen. Simply asking was not enough since Pharaoh did not know the Lord. Therefore, in order to free Israel God poured out plagues upon Egypt. These plagues resulted in the people being set free to worship God. The bowl plagues in Revelation 16 are similar. In six of them we find plagues similar to those found in the plagues on Egypt. There is no reason to believe that these are not literal plagues that will be seen as huge environmental and health disasters. The point of the plagues is similar as well. Through these plagues God will deliver His people. God will set His people apart from the apostate religion in the end, and will reveal His wrath on this apostate religion through the plagues. The result is the battle of Armageddon and the fall of all world governments with the second coming of Jesus Christ.

The second type that is found only in the sixth plague is the fall of Babylon motif. Unlike all the other plagues, the sixth acts as almost an interlude where demonic forces coming from the apostate religion, described as the dragon, beast, and false prophet, go forth to gather the leaders of the world together. Let's look at the text.

> [12] Then the sixth angel poured out his bowl on the great river Euphrates, and its water was dried up, so that the way of the kings from the east might be prepared. [13] And I saw three unclean spirits like frogs *coming* out of the mouth of the dragon, out of the mouth of the beast, and out of the mouth of the false prophet. [14] For they are spirits of demons, performing signs, *which* go out to the kings of the earth and of the whole world, to gather them to the battle of that great day of God Almighty. [15] "Behold, I am coming as a thief. Blessed *is* he who watches, and keeps his garments, lest he walk naked and they see his shame." [16] And they gathered them together to the place called in Hebrew, Armageddon (Revelation 16:12–16, NKJV).

In the prophets Isaiah and Daniel we find the type for which the sixth plague is the antitype. Hundreds of years before it actually took place Isaiah gives multiple prophetic oracles from God regarding the fate of Babylon. The nation of Babylon was used by God as part of the covenant curses against apostate religion dominating Judah towards the end of the reign of the kings. In the 7th century B.C. this proud nation is foreseen by God to have harmed the people much more than God desired, and in Isaiah multiple oracles are leveled against this earthly power (Isaiah 13, 21, 48). God would punish this proud nation for its excess and pride.

The end of Babylon is predicted in advance with amazing accuracy. The prophet Isaiah foresees even the name of the person for whom God will punish Babylon, and the method that this person will use in defeating Babylon. Let's look that the prophetic text.

> 24 Thus says the LORD, your Redeemer, And He who formed you from the womb: "I *am* the LORD, who makes all *things,* Who stretches out the heavens all alone, Who spreads abroad the earth by Myself; 25 Who frustrates the signs of the babblers, And drives diviners mad; Who turns wise men backward, And makes their knowledge foolishness; 26 Who confirms the word of His servant, And performs the counsel of His messengers; Who says to Jerusalem, 'You shall be inhabited,' To the cities of Judah, 'You shall be built,' And I will raise up her waste places; 27 Who says to the deep, 'Be dry! And I will dry up your rivers'; 28 Who says of Cyrus, '*He is* My shepherd, And he shall perform all My pleasure, Saying to Jerusalem, "You shall be built," And to the temple, "Your foundation shall be laid." ' 1 "Thus says the LORD to His anointed, To Cyrus, whose right hand I have held— To subdue nations before him And loose the armor of kings, To open before him the double doors, So that the gates will not be shut (Isaiah 44:24–45:1, NKJV).

This incredible prediction finds its fulfillment in both the books of Daniel and through archaeology and history. Daniel the prophet lived at the time this took place and wrote about it in Daniel chapter 5. In it we find the proud Belshazzar, grandson of Nebuchadnezzar, holding a feast as the armies of the Medes and Persians are outside the city walls. In an act of defiance to God, Belshazzar calls for the holy gold vessels of the temple of the house of God that were carried away from Jerusalem. He defiles them with wine while he praises the idols he trusts. Next, comes God's response as Belshazzar and his party see the handwriting on the wall. Frightened, Belshazzar calls his wise men, and finally a much older Daniel is called who gives the interpretation. Daniel relays that even though Belshazzar knew of God, his pride results in him being weighed and found wanting. He is told that his kingdom will be given to the Medes and Persians. That very night it fell. How it fell is even more interesting.

In the late 19th century, archaeologists discovered an ancient clay cylinder containing Akkadian cuneiform script found in the ruins of the ancient city of Babylon in Mesopotamia. On this cylinder is a document that was issued by Cyrus the Great, the very Persian general who captured Babylon. The document says that Cyrus and his army entered the city without fighting. Ancient historian Herodotus of Halicarnassus (fifth century BC), wrote about how Cyrus was able to accomplish this feat. He writes that Cyrus diverted the river water flowing under the walls of Babylon by building a lake basin upstream. When the water became shallow enough his troops entered under the wall. Amazingly, the city gates that ran along this river were left unlocked, and Cyrus' army entered the city and captured it. The name of this river was the Euphrates. The Cyrus named by the Prophet Isaiah dried up the river Euphrates, went through the double doors that were unlocked, captured Babylon, and allowed the Jews to return to their homeland. Amazing! (Livius.org - Herodotus on Cyrus' capture of Babylon)

The reason I am sharing all this backstory is to point out that the battle of Armageddon in the sixth plague is the antitype. The fall of Babylon in history becomes the type for which the battle of Armageddon is the antitype. As we study the sixth plague and the prophetic account of the battle found in Revelation 17, we need to see the actual fall of Babylon as the stage backdrop for which the fall of spiritual Babylon the Great will take place.

It is also important to realize that the battle of Armageddon is not a literal battle fought in a physical location in modern time. The name itself is also an antitype of a spiritual battle that was fought by Elijah the prophet during the reign of the wicked king Ahab (1 Kings 17-18). We first meet the prophet Elijah as he makes an oath to Ahab that there would be no rain in Israel, except at his word. Three years later the Lord tells Elijah to go and present himself to Ahab. At that time Ahab and a servant in charge of his house were struggling with the effects of the severe drought. As they were out looking for sources of grass that would keep them from having to kill their livestock, suddenly Elijah meets Ahab's servant who brings him to Ahab. Elijah now confronts this wicked king with a challenge.

Elijah declares that the drought was on account of the wicked king who forsook the commandments of the Lord and taught the people to follow the Baals. Now Elijah commands the king to bring all of the prophets of Baal and the prophets of Asherah to meet Elijah on Mount Carmel. Once everyone was assembled, including Ahab and the people of Israel, Elijah makes a challenge to settle matters. He proposes that each side would build an altar and place wood and a sacrifice consisting of a cut up bull upon the altar. Each side would call upon the name of their deity to light the fire and consume the sacrifice. The winning side would be the one whose deity answers by fire to light the wood and burn the sacrifice. Everyone thought this was a good idea, and in the next scene you find the prophets of Baal leaping around their altar, screaming, and cutting themselves. This went on for hours, but there was no voice, no answer, and soon no one paid attention to them.

It was at this point that Elijah asks the people to come near. He wants them to see and participate in what is going to happen next. First, Elijah repairs a broken-down altar for the Lord, he puts wood on it and the sacrifice. Now he challenges the people to help by getting water and pouring it on the offering and wood. So much water was poured upon the altar of the Lord that it was filling the trench around it with water. The time was now when Israel would have offered the evening sacrifice at the temple in Jerusalem, and Elijah speaks to the Lord, that the hearts of the people would turn back to the Lord. ROAR! Fire falls from heaven in the sight of men. It disintegrates absolutely everything, and the people shout: "The Lord, He is God."

Scholars have determined that the mysterious name Armageddon is a compound word that means mountain of Megiddo. The ancient city of Megiddo is in what is called the Jezreel Valley, or valley of Megiddo. It is a fertile inland plain located in northern Israel. This valley also was strategically important as the crossroads for both military and commercial trade routes. Mount Carmel, the place of the great spiritual battle in Elijah's day, is a mountain range that runs along the northeast side of the Valley of Jezreel. The mountain of Megiddo would be the Mount Carmel range. The great spiritual battle fought there by Elijah against the prophets of Baal now serves as a type for the final spiritual gathering called Armageddon, that takes place at the time of the 6th plague.

The place called Armageddon in the sixth plague serves as the antitype to the great spiritual battle fought there by Elijah against the prophets of Baal. Armageddon is not a literal battle fought in modern Israel. As the antitype

Armageddon asks us to remember the back story of the great spiritual battle fought there by Elijah. As the antitype it becomes the stage backdrop for us to imagine the end-time battle on the earth over who is God. That battle begins long before the final gathering at Armageddon in the sixth plague. It begins with Revelation 12:17, where the dragon (the devil) is now at war with a new threat. The dragon at this time is unconcerned with popular Christianity. Instead, at the end, this dragon goes after the remnant of the Christian church who have two unique characteristics. They keep God's commandments and they have the testimony of Jesus, which is revealed in Chapter 19 to be the Spirit of Prophecy. In other words, they have a true prophetic witness in contrast to the false prophet of the sixth plague. Chapters 13 and 14 then reveal the players that will come together at the end.

Revelation chapter 13 provides the lineage of the two major powers that combine in the 6th plague. The first is the sea beast who, having the animal elements of Daniel 7's beasts in reverse order, is none other than the Papacy that arose out of the Roman Empire and received its power, seat, and great authority from it by the dragon. This is the same dragon who is seen using the power of Rome as a means of killing the Messiah in chapter 12. We find the 1260 day/year reign of this power, its deadly wound, and its miraculous resurrection at the end. It is stated plainly here that when the world worships the papacy, it is actually worshipping the dragon (Revelation 13:4). Also like the little horn found in Daniel 7, this power speaks great boasts, blaspheming God, and persecuting the saints. This power is the beast referred to in the sixth plague. Even with all its power, it still needs help to carry out its goals. Let's look at its helper.

Revelation 13:11 begins the identification of another world power coming up out of the earth looking like an innocent two horned lamb, but speaking like a dragon. Many scholars have seen this as Protestant America. It rose in the century that the papacy received its deadly wound. Its birth was not in the waters of Europe, but in a new land. Protestant America was also born with freedom from the oppression of king and pope. Its founding demanded no state religion. However, Revelation 13 shows that at the end it will join itself again to the papacy. The last day deception that will draw the world to the papacy will come out of Protestant America. It is called the false prophet in the sixth plague.

> 12 And he exerciseth all the power of the first beast before him, and causeth the earth and them which dwell therein to worship the first beast, whose deadly wound was healed. 13 And he doeth great wonders, so that he maketh fire come down from heaven on the earth in the sight of men, 14 And deceiveth them that dwell on the earth by *the means of* those miracles which he had power to do in the sight of the beast; saying to them that dwell on the earth, that they should make an image to the beast, which had the wound by a sword, and did live (Revelation 13:12–14, KJV).

Revelation 13:12 reveals that Protestant America will copy the type of control that the sea beast possessed during its 1260-year reign. It will use it to enforce worship that honors the sea beast. All of this is done through deception. Here we find the great antitype of Elijah's battle over who is God. Here false charisma makes it seem that fire is coming down from heaven, but it falls on the wrong altar! The people of the earth are deceived by this false charisma, enabling Protestant America to toss its founding documents aside as it speaks like a dragon. Protestant America will become the driving force in forcing the world to worship the image of the sea beast and take its mark and number. With this introduction in Revelation chapter 12 and 13, we are made aware of the false trinity – dragon, sea beast and false prophet, through which the spirits of demon's work to gather the whole world together to the great battle of God found in the interlude of the sixth bowl plague. The question now is where in the Revelation is the battle fought, and what are the results?

Chapter 7

Is Armageddon Really a Good Thing?

Armageddon can be described as a gathering together of world leaders led by demonic-backed religious forces. To the average person this gathering will appear without the knowledge of who is behind it all. They will just see people who desire to form a new world order. They might even let it slip that their plan comes from a source that is almost extraterrestrial. Regardless of how it is perceived, it will succeed. You would not believe it even if you were told, but the reason it will succeed is because God has been behind it all along. In this chapter we will look at the final players in the battle of Armageddon, the play action, and the final result.

THE JUDGMENT HOUR HAS ARRIVED

The place where Armageddon is fought is found in Revelation 17. Right away we are told the reason for the whole affair. It is a judgment on apostate Christianity. This is revealed in the introduction of this chapter.

> ¹ And there came one of the seven angels which had the seven vials, and talked with me, saying unto me, Come hither; I will shew unto thee the judgment of the great whore that sitteth upon many waters: ² With whom the kings of the earth have committed fornication, and the inhabitants of the earth have

been made drunk with the wine of her fornication (Revelation 17:1–2, KJV).

The judgment of Babylon mirrors the judgments ancient Israel faced and the root cause of their failure. Very early in the history of Israel you find their backsliding. Israel was to be faithful and loyal to their Creator who redeemed them. However, with the death of Joshua who brought them into the land God promised to Abraham, their hearts turned from God and towards the nations round about them. By using the word "fornication," a New Testament term, we are drawn into the Old Testament imagery of adultery. Israel's backsliding first began by desiring other nations. This desire for their people and culture was seen by God as illicit sexual activity, which always resulted in their choosing the gods of those nations.

Consider the prophet Hosea. He is commanded to take a wife of whoredoms, "for the land had committed great whoredom, departing from the Lord" (Hosea 1:2). They are discovered in the very act of fornication with their lovers, and believe that the abundance of blessings God poured out on them actually came from the false gods their neighbors worshiped (Hosea 2:6-13). The result of this fornication is a loss of the knowledge of God and an adoption of the ways of their neighbors. This always resulted in the people breaking the covenant document, the Ten Commandments (Hosea 4:1-2). This fornication resulted in God's chosen people committing unspeakable acts of brutality (Ezekiel 16:36). When the judgment hour arrived for Israel and Judah, it was the prophets Jeremiah and Ezekiel who summarized the situation as a desire for the culture of the foreign kings whom they committed fornication with (Ezekiel 23).

This imagery of adultery in Revelation 17 is applied to the papacy (sea beast) and apostate Protestantism (false prophet). Judgment upon these Apostates is the subject of the battle of Armageddon. If you look at the history of Christianity, it did not take long for the early church to commit fornication with the culture present in the Roman Empire. It happened as the church left the Synagogue culture in the second century. The popular early church fathers sniffed after the Hellenistic view of God and man. Their use of Greek philosophy to describe God, man, and the creation resulted in a transformation of belief that exists still today. Not long after that, the emperor Constantine adopted Christianity and molded it into the structure of the Roman Empire. This fornication resulted in adopting the desires and culture of the Romans that only intensified as the papacy was born. Led by Neoplatonist theologians like Augustine of Hippo and his dream of using state power to conquer the world for Jesus by force, the image of apostate religion sitting upon the backs of government becomes reality. Prophecy in Revelation 13 and Daniel 7 reveals that this always results in heinous atrocities committed on innocents. People considered to be heretics by the papacy were killed by the millions as the papacy is given a license to kill by her fornication with world governments.

The Protestant reformation reacted to the excesses and sinful practices of the papacy. It was enabled by access to the Scriptures. The great names of reformers who risked all to bring the Bible to the people brought needed reform, but many of the reformers only went so far. They kept the Hellenism of earlier years and it weakened them from completing the reformation. They kept the structure of the Roman Empire and the sun day worshiped by Constantine. These failures in reform would eventually lead these same Protestants to adopt the culture of atheistic evolution in the 19th and 20th centuries.

The Protestant churches, like Judah before them, also sought after the culture around them. With the help of the papacy, many today openly lust after the theory of evolution. They seek the culture of the nations and believe that it reveals the works of God. They fornicate with the kings of this earth to adopt practices that the Bible calls abominations. Like Judah, they do this with abandon. Once again, a great need to return to the Scriptures is required, but as the time of this great judgment nears few heed the prophetic cries to "come out of her My people" (Revelation 18:4). Apostate Protestantism, aided by false charisma rejoins with the mother church, and through this union it leads the world to worship the beast who received the deadly wound, that now has miraculously been resurrected. Something has gone wrong, and as the Protestant church views the 1260 years of papal dominance in the rear-view mirror it begins to change to the point that it no longer is a threat to the dragon. Instead, in this final spiritual and world-wide apostasy the dragon's battle is with the remnant of the Protestant church that "keep the commandments of God, and have the testimony of Jesus" (Revelation 12:17; Revelation 14:12).

UNDERSTANDING THE PLAYERS AND TIMING IN THIS LAST GREAT BATTLE

The next scenes in Revelation 17 provides an introduction to the players in this final battle against God.

> 3 So he carried me away in the Spirit into the wilderness. And I saw a woman sitting on a scarlet beast *which was* full of names of blasphemy, having seven heads and ten horns. 4 The woman was arrayed in purple and scarlet, and adorned with gold and precious stones and pearls, having in her hand a golden cup full of abominations and the

filthiness of her fornication. [5] And on her forehead a name *was* written: MYSTERY, BABYLON THE GREAT, THE MOTHER OF HARLOTS AND OF THE ABOMINATIONS OF THE EARTH [6] I saw the woman, drunk with the blood of the saints and with the blood of the martyrs of Jesus. And when I saw her, I marveled with great amazement (Revelation 17:3–6, NKJV).

It is significant that John is taken into the wilderness to see this last manifestation of the dragon's battle against Christ. Revelation 12 can be likened to the dragon's war against Christ. It begins with the birth of Christ where the dragon waits to kill the child at His birth. This fails, but eventually the dragon succeeds by hanging Jesus on the cross. However, this fails as Jesus is resurrected the third day, and ascends into heaven where the dragon is again defeated and thrown to the earth with all his followers. Next, we find this period of 1260 years where the dragon goes after the Messiah's followers. God helps them across water to a place of safety, and then we hear nothing until finally the dragon goes after the remnant of this woman. I find it interesting that in each of these three periods, the focus is on the dragon's work to destroy the Messiah's ministry and message by attacking His people. By taking us into the wilderness to see this final abomination, we are led to find the power through which the dragon persecuted the church in the wilderness – The sea beast of Revelation 13 – the papacy.

The image that is described above of the woman sitting on the beast is identical to what occurred during the 1260-year reign of the papacy (538-1798 AD). In Revelation 13 this relationship is simply described as the sea beast, but a similar arrangement is found. During the dark ages, the papacy was integrated into the governments of Europe. It was the state religion. It was the papacy that was seen giving these kings their legitimacy, and opposing those who got out of line. The papal state was useful to these kings, providing them with docile subjects and serving as a security service through the confessional to root out detractors. The papacy also benefitted from the state, receiving taxes, and by being given a free hand to capture, torture, and kill anyone that did not conform. It is this period in history that we are to bring to mind as we are taken to see the harlot Babylon riding upon the nations of the world at the end.

The difference between the beast the harlot rode during the wilderness period and the beast at the end is seen in its color (the same as the dragon in Revelation 12) and the many names of blasphemy that are written upon it. Unlike the kings that supported the papacy these kings are unbelievers. The Greek word blasphemy is generally used for any kind of speech that is defamatory or abusive, that reviles, disrespects, or slanders (BDAG, βλασφημία). This word specifically is used in the New Testament when the abuse is directed towards God. You would not expect the kings during the 1260-year papal reign to revile God this way. There was at least a pretense that they were worshippers of God. What this shows us is the fact that the world powers in the final ride of apostate Babylon are secular powers. They do not believe. This is seen in the disrespect, slander, and abuse the biblical followers of Jesus experience at the hands of these governments and their surrogates. Already throughout the world, biblical faith and belief is not appreciated by the secular governments of today.

The question we need to ask is how can any form of the Christian religion sit on a secular beast? The answer is they can't unless they have something they agree upon.

The thing that both the papacy and apostate Protestantism have in common with the secular world is found in their belief in origins. All of them have adopted the false theory of origins that denies everything that the Bible says about God. In the Bible from start to finish, God is seen as our Creator; the One who made the heavens, the earth, and all life. Nothing that we see is an accident. It was designed. It was planned, and it was implemented. However, the secular world desires a secular god; one that takes star dust and uses the magic of time and chance to create what we see. It is total myth. The theory of evolution may have been chosen by secular scientists, but it flies in the face of empirical science. The very existence of the information in DNA, the irreducibly complex machines that read it, and the micro machines that are programmed by it to create proteins, flies in the face of the discredited theories of Darwin. Yet, these beliefs are chosen specifically because they deny the Creator of the Bible. If God is Creator, then God's rules apply. If not, then the world can ignore the Ten Commandments. If you are paying attention, you will notice that they ignore every single one of them. In the end, the reason that the papacy and apostate Protestantism, or any other religion that unites with them can sit on the secular red beast is because they agree in both origins and in morality.

A contemporary illustration of this is found in communist China. In 2018 the Vatican and China signed a historic agreement on the appointment of Roman Catholic bishops in China. The result of the agreement gave Beijing authority to appoint bishops without the need for Vatican approval. The spin from the Vatican was that this new arrangement will create conditions for greater collaboration.[5] This agreement, which has been renewed in recent years, is an example of what I have been referring. This is exactly what Old Testament Israel did in joining itself with pagan nations and is a hallmark of the papacy. The practical result of the agreement is the recognition of the papacy in China. Protestants, however, have suffered from this agreement. Many of the public Protestant churches in China have had their properties demolished, their leaders detained, and many have gone underground as a result. In Henan province, the local authorities required churches to remove the first commandment from the list of the Ten Commandments on the grounds that it placed loyalty to God above loyalty to the CCP.[6] In the end, Babylon will once again be seen sitting upon world governments, even communist ones. Revelation 17 now reveals the timing for the dragon's last battle.

It is not surprising that John was astonished by what he had just seen. In response the angel now provides additional clues to unpack the timing of the dragon's last battle with the remnant church.

> [7] And the angel said unto me, Wherefore didst thou marvel? I will tell thee the mystery of the woman, and of the beast that carrieth her, which hath the seven heads and ten horns. [8] The beast that thou sawest was, and is not; and shall ascend out of the bottomless pit, and go into perdition: and they that dwell on the earth shall wonder, whose names were not written in the book of life from the foundation of the world, when they behold the beast that was,

[5] The Guardian online; Vatican Signs historic deal with China – but critics denounce sellout; September 22, 2018.
[6] Angeline Tan; Why the CCP Fears Christianity; The Roseburg Beacon; January 18-24, 2023.

and is not, and yet is. ⁹ And here *is* the mind which hath wisdom. The seven heads are seven mountains, on which the woman sitteth. ¹⁰ And there are seven kings: five are fallen, and one is, *and* the other is not yet come; and when he cometh, he must continue a short space. ¹¹ And the beast that was, and is not, even he is the eighth, and is of the seven, and goeth into perdition (Revelation 17:7–11, KJV).

A couple of points to keep in mind as you consider the text you just read. First, you are seeing the last manifestation of the kind of power the papacy wielded in the past. Second, this harlot is described as sitting on many waters. The many waters we learn later, are people, multitudes, nations, and tongues (Revelation 17:15). This shows us that we are not talking about a literal beast, but rather a combination of world governments. It is the governments that are in view. With this in mind, it is easier to unravel the mystery.

The first clue to unravel the timing of this last event is found in the statement: "The beast that you saw was and is not, and will ascend out of the bottomless pit and go to perdition." Since we are looking at the last manifestation of church/state power, we only need to look backwards to see when governments enabled the Sea Beast and when they did not. See Figure 9, below.

In Figure 9 we find a timeline that begins with the 1260 years of papal dominance that is recorded in Daniel 7 and in Revelation 12 & 13. This is the "was," state represented by the sea beast of Revelation 13. In this "was" state the governments of Europe are seen as the beast power that supported the papacy. The papacy received a deadly wound as indicated earlier when Napoleon removed the temporal power from the papacy in 1798 AD. This begins the next phase which is the "is not" phase. In this phase the papacy does not have the kind of temporal power that it once wielded over the nations of Europe. Even though the temporal power of the papacy has been restored in the Lateran Treaty, it is still not at the level of power described in Revelation 17. In this "is not" phase the papacy acts like a government on the earth. It gives and receives ambassadors and has a seat at the United Nations. It is treated as a world power, and it is certainly true that all the world is wondering after it. However, it currently is not being supported by the governments of the earth. This changes in the final "is about to come" phase. In this phase the beast that comes out of the bottomless pit supports the final manifestation of the union of the papacy with secular world governments at the end. Thankfully, we see the end of this beast is near. But first, God has something for it to do.

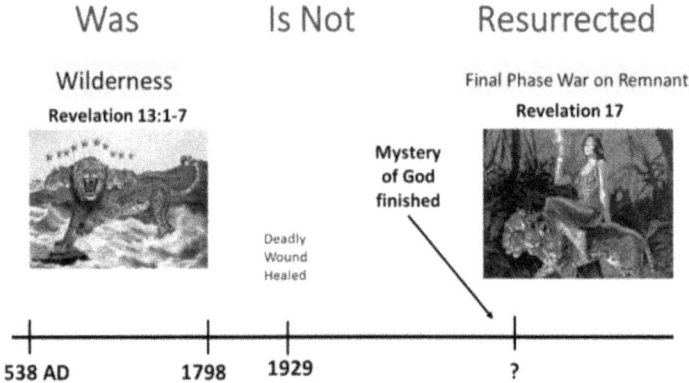

Figure 9.

The next clue will come in the form of heads, mountains, and kings. Once again, we are asked to visualize the beast that supports this kind of arrangement of a religion/state power that oppresses God's people in historical terms. It becomes clearer when we go back to Revelation 12 and look at the origin of the characteristics of the beasts we find in Revelation 13 and 17. In chapter 12 we are introduced to the fiery red dragon. It is described as a beast with seven heads and ten horns, with kingly crowns on each of the heads. We later learn that this beast is the devil himself. What this implies is the fact that the devil uses world governments in his fight against God's purposes. In Revelation 12 we find that the specific head the devil was using to attack the Messiah was the Roman Empire. These seven heads represent world powers through which the devil fights against God's purposes and oppresses God's people. Next, notice that all the beasts that come after it have the same characteristics, except for where the crowns are located. In the sea beast they are located on the ten horns, connecting us to Daniel 7 and the rise of the papacy out of the ten divisions of the western Roman empire. In Revelation 17 you will notice that there are no crowns. These governments are not kingdoms but some form of representative government as we have today.

These seven heads become a key to unlock the meaning of the seven mountains/kings leading to the final red beast that supports religious Babylon. All of them represent the merging of religious-state power. All oppressed God's people in the past, and will again in the future. See Figure 10.

By allowing the seven heads to represent the seven mountains and kings we find a history of kingdoms that fought against God's purposes and oppressed God's people. If the one that "is" represents the power that existed when John received his vision, it would be the Roman empire. The five that have fallen trace their lineage from Egyptian to Greece. The one that "was and is not" represents the papacy in both its sea beast phase, and after it received its deadly wound. The final miraculous resurrection combining the papacy with the secular red beast, now becomes the eight head, and was one of the seven. In other words, it has the same characteristics. During the reign of the sea beast, it was the governments of Europe that were seen supporting the papacy. In the final phase this type of arrangement is resurrected, except this time it is world-wide in scope.

The Beasts of Revelation 12 & 17 Compared

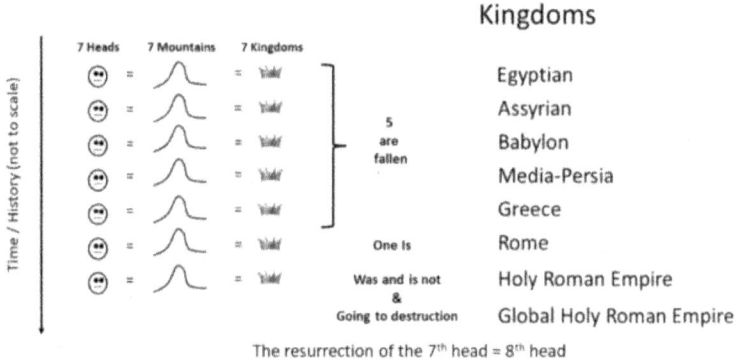

Figure 10.

THE FINAL MOVEMENTS IN THE BATTLE OF ARMAGEDDON

The next thing that John is told regarding this last manifestation of religion/state power is that its purpose is to attack the Lamb. But this attack will backfire. Attacking the Lamb is realized by persecuting Christ's end-time remnant. These are the ones the Dragon is furious with because they keep God's commandments and have God's testimony (Revelation 12:17). To this small group things seem dire, but this process actually separates the people of the world into two groups. Some will heed the last-day messages of Revelation 14, and others will worship the image of the beast and take its mark and its number. It looks as if this miraculous joining of world governments is going to succeed. The Dragon will finally receive what he desires, worship. As the populations of the world align themselves, they will either worship the Dragon through this merging of Babylon with the red beast, or they will worship our Creator, who made the heavens, and the earth, and the fountains of waters (Revelation 14:6-13). This becomes the stage for the final battle of Armageddon. Fortunately for God's people, the battle belongs to the Lord. The red beast is going to fail spectacularly. Now we discover that this gathering of world leaders was God's purpose all along. Let's look at the play-by-play action.

> 12 "The ten horns which you saw are ten kings who have received no kingdom as yet, but they receive authority for one hour as kings with the beast. 13 These are of one mind, and they will give their power and authority to the beast. 14 These will make war with the Lamb, and the Lamb will overcome them, for He is Lord of lords and King of kings; and those *who are* with Him *are* called, chosen, and faithful" (Revelation 17:12–14, NKJV).

We have ten kings that have no kingdoms. But with the support of the beast, they start acting like kings. This is describing the coming together of world governments that will ultimately support the harlot woman. At some point there will be rulers in this confederation that will begin to act like kings. I find it interesting that there are two organizations currently that mirror what we find in this text. The first is the United Nations. It is an organization of world government that will represent the beast that will support the harlot woman in the end. The second is an organization currently called the World Economic Forum (WEF). It consists of believers in a new world order that will unite world governments into a scheme that is a partnership of transnational globalist corporations and similar entities, with world governments. It is a secular organization that sees China and its form of communist-styled capitalism as the model for world governance. The WEF desires corporations, governments, and other globalist entities to become stakeholders with one another, to the exclusion of citizens and shareholders. Using the United Nations originated global warming threat and the recent man-made global pandemic, this organization has made incredible strides to make this goal a reality.

This gathering of world governments is backed by demonic religious forces. One of the key players in this gathering is the papacy. It is seen time and again as the agitator for the need to come together to solve global warming. The papacy has also taken the lead in calling for a world religion. Along with the meetings of world leaders there are meetings of world religions. Again, the papacy is seen as the leader. There is a desire to create a world religion. A religion that takes what they consider the best qualities of each. A world religion that will be led by the papacy and will one day sit upon the red beast at the end and demand the worship of the peoples of the world.

World leaders that come out of the World Economic Forum have also acted like kings in recent years. We find that during the global pandemic, democracies became dictatorships, as the president or prime minister became authoritarian, denying their citizens their basic rights by confiscating their bank accounts if they protest. We have seen the rise of a new kind of leader elected to serve over a democratically elected government, but following the dictates of the globalist cabal. I am not saying that this is the fulfillment of the prophecy, but it sure makes for a good illustration of what is coming.

Ultimately, the goal of bringing together this body of world governments is to allow the harlot to sit upon it once again. This will bring in a world religion, a religion that is good for the environment, but without all the biblical morality of a Creator with Ten Commandments. Something like this is already in the works. Meetings of world religions headed by the papacy, to derive what they consider the best from each that will serve as the basis of the world religion that the papacy will ultimately lead.

The Confederation of religion and state power has a purpose. Just as in the case of the sea beast, it is to lead people to worship the image of the beast, and in the process give worship to the dragon. This is the war that is implied in the prophecy. This war is also seen in Revelation 13, where the image of the beast is to be worshiped and people are to take its mark and the number of its name. Again, the battle is over worship. Who is God?

The remnant described in Revelation 14 have the answer to that question. This group is given the message of the three angels. Their response to this question is a gospel message that calls people to fear God, give Him glory, and worship Him who made the heavens, and the earth and the seas, and the springs of waters. Their cry is to return to the biblical worship found in the fourth commandment. At a time when this world cabal is featuring Sunday as a World Day of Rest to save the planet, the remnant will be calling for true worship, worship that declares that our God is the Creator. The battle at the end is about worship. The dragon desires it, but only God deserves it.

The world at this time will be forced to choose between that pesky remnant versus the world government and its harlot religion. There will be calls for national Sunday closing laws, and these laws will increase in their strictness until it becomes a mark that proves where your loyalty lies. Will it be the secular beast and the harlot that rides upon it, or will it be the biblical Creator, Jesus? In the end people will be forced to choose. This is why the next two messages of the three angels are so important.

The second and third messages contains strong warnings to the people of the earth. Babylon is fallen, it is fallen! The harlot and her daughters present to the world a fallen religion; one that has committed fornication with the kings of the earth. It sounds good, but it is compromised. It directs worship to the resurrected sea beast, and through it to the dragon. The final message becomes a warning to the people of the earth. If anyone worships the beast, or its image, or takes its mark, they will drink from the wine of God's wrath. What will you do? God will allow the people of the world to make that choice. However, prophecy shows us who will win this battle. In one simple phrase the prophecy says Jesus wins again. The next thing that occurs is a description of the destruction of Babylon.

> 15 Then he said to me, "The waters which you saw, where the harlot sits, are peoples, multitudes, nations, and tongues. 16 And the ten horns which you saw on the beast, these will hate the harlot, make her desolate and naked, eat her flesh and burn her with fire. 17 For God has put it into their hearts to fulfill His purpose, to be of one mind, and to give their kingdom to the beast, until the words of God are fulfilled. 18 And the woman whom you saw is that great city which reigns over the kings of the earth" (Revelation 17:15–18, NKJV).

Did you see that coming? The utter destruction of Babylon by the lovers she lusted over? At the end, the papacy, apostate Protestantism, and the other world religions that unite with the papacy will all be caught up in the net and destroyed. The imagery in this text reveals the battle of Armageddon as God's judgment on apostate Christianity. This is not something new, it has been foretold in the Scriptures. Consider the following example.

> 35 'Now then, O harlot, hear the word of the LORD! 36 Thus says the Lord GOD: "Because your filthiness was poured out and your nakedness uncovered in your harlotry with your lovers, and with all your abominable idols, and because of the blood of your children which you gave to them, 37 surely, therefore, I will gather all your lovers with whom you took pleasure, all those you loved, *and* all those you hated; I will gather them from all around against you and will uncover your nakedness to them, that they may see all your nakedness. 38 And I will judge you as women who break wedlock or shed blood are judged; I will bring blood upon you in fury and jealousy. 39 I will also give you into their hand, and they shall throw down your shrines and break down your high places. They shall also strip you of your clothes, take your beautiful jewelry, and leave you naked and bare. 40 "They shall also bring up an assembly against you, and they shall stone you with stones and thrust you through with their swords. 41 They shall burn your houses with fire, and execute judgments on you in the sight of many women; and I will make you cease playing the harlot, and you shall no longer hire lovers. 42 So I will lay to rest My fury toward you, and My jealousy shall depart from you. I will be quiet, and be angry no more (Ezekiel 16:35–42, NKJV).

This gathering of world governments led by demonic backed forces is inevitable. Suddenly, in Revelation 17:17

we find that God was behind it all along. God put it into their hearts to join together for a short season. God was behind their drive to have this common purpose. This movement all along was designed to bring the whole world to this conclusion. In the end the plagues that fall are all directed to the harlot and her lovers. The failure of this religion/state to combat them brings us to this Battle of Armageddon. The world suddenly realizes they have been deceived and turns on the religion that was riding their back. The world then experiences its final movements as the people, without restraint, await the soon coming of the Lord of lord's and King of kings. See Figure 11 for a summary of the battle of Armageddon.

It turns out that Armageddon is actually a good thing. First, through it God preserves his remnant. Second, it will not last long. In multiple texts we are told that it will continue only a short time. It will be in one day. It will be in one hour (Revelation 17:9, 18:8, 18:17). Unlike the long reign of the papacy for 1260 years, this final manifestation of church/state power will only last a short season. Even though the events that bring all this together may take some time, the actual battle will not last long.

Why Armageddon is a good thing

Revelation 17

The Battle Belongs to the Lord!

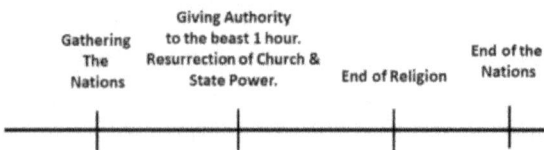

Gathering The Nations	Giving Authority to the beast 1 hour. Resurrection of Church & State Power.	End of Religion	End of the Nations

Figure 11.

This is good news for God's faithful as they remember the words of the prophet Isaiah. "Come, my people, enter thou into thy chambers, And shut thy doors about thee: Hide thyself as it were for a little moment, Until the indignation be overpast" (Isaiah 26:20, KJV). The final indignation is coming upon the whole world, and now with the end of religion, the world heaves as we watch the devil's final moments before the Second Coming of the Messiah. We will study what that world will look like next.

Chapter 8

World on Fire!
The Great Time of Trouble

In this chapter we will look at the influences in the world that become the embers that ignite the flames of a great time of trouble. This study will cover the major movements both from a historical and prophetic perspective. Both will illustrate the direction the world is heading at the end, and what things will look like as Babylon falls. In the process we will look at the two indignations and how events during the French Revolution will telegraph the world events that shape the final movements of earth's history.

A PROPHETIC ILLUSTRATION – The French Revolution

In the eleventh chapter of the book of Revelation we are shown events that transpired during the reign of the sea beast. Here you find a reference of the 42 months, or 1260 days/years, period of its reign. During this time there is a need for heavenly help to preserve what is being corrupted by the sea beast. At the end something happens. A new power rises that grows in the ensuing century to leaven the cultural, and political substance that will one day make up the scarlet beast that will support the harlot Babylon when the end comes. For this reason, it becomes an important subject for our knowledge of end events.

> [1] And there was given me a reed like unto a rod: and the angel stood, saying, Rise, and measure the

temple of God, and the altar, and them that worship therein. ² But the court which is without the temple leave out, and measure it not; for it is given unto the Gentiles: and the holy city shall they tread under foot forty *and* two months (Revelation 11:1–2 KJV).

The Sanctuary

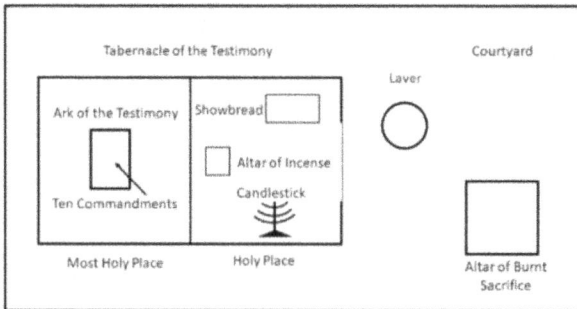

Figure 12.

The events John is shown taking place here are located in the Sanctuary in heaven. These events are not taking place on the earth. At this time, the Jerusalem temple has been in ruins for centuries. Earlier, in Chapter 4, John was asked to come up to heaven, and the events that take place after this are either in heaven, or on the earth as seen from that heavenly location (Revelation 4:1). What John is viewing at this time is the Sanctuary in heaven, the one that Moses saw when he was shown the pattern and made the earthly one (Hebrews 8). See Figure 12.

In this prophetic imagery we find that something is being preserved and something is being let go during the 42 prophetic months of the sea beast's reign. What is being preserved is found in the parts of the Sanctuary that are being measured. This would be the Tabernacle of the Testimony. This is the place where Jesus our High Priest would be ministering the New Covenant in His blood. Just as in the Old Testament Sanctuary, this is the location where the bread of life is found, the prayers of the saints, depicted by the incense, and the Spirit who brings light to the faithful. It is also the place where the throne of God is located, depicted as the Ark of the Testimony. It is a sacred place, and now is being measured so as to preserve it during the 42 months.

The courtyard is discarded and left to the gentiles to trample. What an apt description of the theological mischief that occurred during the dark ages. At this time the papacy invented the mass to replace Jesus' ministry of atonement. This was figured by the altar of burnt sacrifice, where the daily burnt sacrifice of Daniel 8 is declared to be attacked by the little horn during this 1260-year period (Daniel 8:9-14). In this period the mediatorial role of Jesus in heaven is replace by sinful men that the people are taught to call Father. In this period salvation can be purchased with indulgences, and penances. Truly, from a heavenly perspective the courtyard is being trampled under-foot.

Next God pronounces that during this horrible period the Scriptures will be guarded.

> 3 And I will give *power* unto my two witnesses, and they shall prophesy a thousand two hundred *and* threescore days, clothed in sackcloth. 4 These are the two olive trees, and the two candlesticks standing before the God of the earth. 5 And if any man will hurt them, fire proceedeth out of their mouth, and devoureth their enemies: and if any man will hurt them, he must in this manner be killed. 6 These have power to shut heaven, that it rain not in the days of their prophecy: and have power over waters to turn them to blood, and to smite the earth with all plagues, as often as they will (Revelation 11:3–6, KJV).

Now we see what made the Protestant Reformation possible. God preserved His word! The Old and New Testaments are the two witnesses described in verses 3-6. These prophesy in sackcloth during the 1260 day/years of papal reign. God made special efforts in this time to ensure that the Bible would be preserved for the Protestant Reformation. It is God's two witnesses that are still a prophetic witness to us today. Aren't you thankful that God has preserved them for you?

THE FIRST INDIGNATION

Next the prophecy shows us that something is coming that has demonic origins. It will make an attack against God and His word. This power rises on the world stage at the end of the 1260 years of the Bible's testimony in sackcloth. Let's look at the play by play.

> 7 And when they shall have finished their testimony, the beast that ascendeth out of the bottomless pit shall make war against them, and shall overcome them, and kill them. 8 And their dead bodies *shall lie* in the street of the great city, which spiritually is called Sodom and Egypt, where also our Lord was crucified. 9 And they of the people and kindreds and tongues and nations shall see their dead bodies three days and an half, and shall not suffer their dead bodies to be put in graves. 10 And they that dwell upon the earth shall rejoice over them, and make merry, and shall send gifts one to another; because these two prophets tormented them that dwelt on the earth. 11 And after three days and an half the Spirit of life from God entered into them, and they stood upon their feet; and great fear fell upon them which saw them. 12 And they heard a

great voice from heaven saying unto them, Come up hither. And they ascended up to heaven in a cloud; and their enemies beheld them (Revelation 11:7–12 KJV).

Every time the bottomless pit, or abyss, is mentioned in the Revelation, it always describes something that deals with the demonic. Here, and in Revelation 17:8, we find that a power enters the world that has one purpose, to kill God's prophetic witness. It is an atheistic, and immoral power that enters the world, and infects its culture and politics. It will ultimately be seen as the scarlet beast with names of blasphemy that supports the final manifestation of the resurrected sea beast in its quest for world domination.

The timing for the rise of this demonic power is described as being at the end of the testimony of the two witnesses. If we look in history for such a power rising upon the earth, we find it in the French Revolution. See Figure 13.

Timeline for the rise of an Atheistic Power

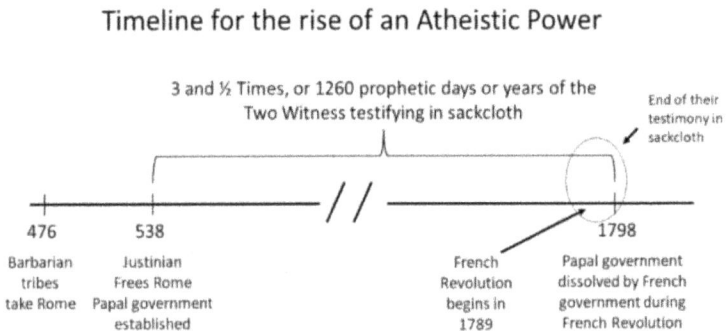

Figure 13.

Towards the end of the 1260-year prophecy, a revolution was brewing in Catholic France. It was unforeseen by the papacy or the government. It was a revolution that created a new government, and in the process birthed an atheistic and secular humanist worldview. By studying the French Revolution, we can discern a pattern that has been repeated again and again over time.

A demonic world power was now coming on the scene, one that is unique in its hatred for the God of the Bible. Through this power a proclamation was issued. In the midst of the French Revolution, it was proclaimed that "God is not the Creator, and the Bible is not to be followed anymore." This is the first indignation, and it has resonated in the world ever since. Prophecy indicates that before the coming of Christ there will be a final indignation. This time it will be a world-wide proclamation. It is for this reason we need to study this important period to discern its structure and to understand how all this could take place. Figure 14 outlines the basic parts of the French Revolution.

The French Revolution is the model for the Communist Revolutions that followed in the 20ᵗʰ Century

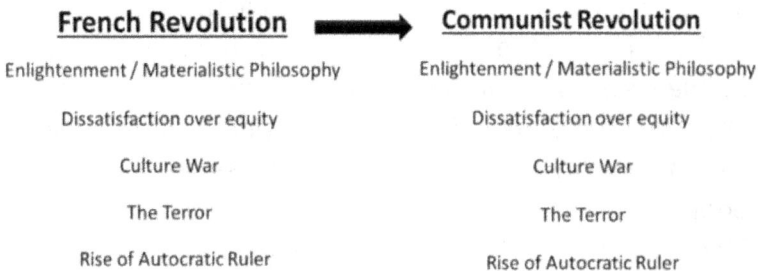

French Revolution ➡	Communist Revolution
Enlightenment / Materialistic Philosophy	Enlightenment / Materialistic Philosophy
Dissatisfaction over equity	Dissatisfaction over equity
Culture War	Culture War
The Terror	The Terror
Rise of Autocratic Ruler	Rise of Autocratic Ruler

Figure 14.

The French Revolution could be outlined as having five parts. The first consists of the cultural movement called the Enlightenment with its materialistic philosophers.

85

Long before there was a revolution in France, there were changing attitudes that were happening throughout Europe. A simple description of the Enlightenment would be to describe it as an era of advances in science, technology, and philosophy that allows smaller numbers of people to have a greater influence. In the century of the revolution there were numerous advances that enabled fewer people to have an enormous impact. For example, the metric system was developed that allowed standardization in production and commerce. It was the time of the rise of factories and techniques to make steel, and advanced methods of producing gun powder which enabled the use of new weapons for war. It was the time of incredible advances in mathematics and science with Lagrange and Laplace that revealed a stable universe. There were also advances in medicine that prevented war wounds from becoming fatal. This era saw new techniques to combat infection with the proper treatment of injury.

Another area of the Enlightenment that had the greatest impact to society was the advances in the production of books. It has been recorded that in France books were everywhere on every subject imaginable. Besides the Bible, which sparked the Protestant Reformation, the ability to mass produce books also gave the materialistic philosophers of the age the ability to influence the masses. In *The French Revolution* historian Louis Madelin writes about the three main French philosophers whose ideas were penetrating the culture by the mass production of books. They are Montesquieu, Voltaire, and Rousseau. Madelin remarks that "Every one of them bears the impress of the same philosophy – a purely destructive philosophy be it said" (Madelin, p14). Then being more specific about how the teachings of these philosophers was destructive to society, he gives a summary of their characteristics. He writes:

All were from the intellectual College crowd that could be described as: ideological dogmatism, classicism, cosmopolitanism, humanitarianism, anti-Christianism, and a philosophism destructive to all authority (Madelin, p15).

For us to discern this important statement we need to start by looking at the characteristics of these ideas coming from the higher educational centers of France. Each one will reveal something that was changing the society in a major way, and enabling the dramatic changes that were coming.

TEACHINGS THAT LED TO THE FRENCH REVOLUTION

The first teaching is called "ideological dogmatism." This describes people who possess ideas that they feel are absolute, and they are absolutely unwilling to debate about them. There is no way to reason with a person like this. "I am right, you are wrong, period!" "Nothing you have to say has any validity unless it agrees with me." If you are living in second decade of the 21st century you will instantly recognize what is implied by ideological dogmatism. In this decade there are ideas that have been coming from the college crowd that are now considered dogma. There can be absolutely no room for debate, and if you disagree publicly you are shamed, or worse.

In our century, these ideas are inclusive in the word "Woke," and convey a spectrum of dogmatic ideas that you are not allowed to publicly refute. A sample of Woke dogmas includes beliefs that promote pro-LGBTQ+, pro-transgenderism, pro-extreme racism, man-made global warming, anti-conservatism, anti-Bible, pro-Marxist, pro-criminal, anti-life, anti-patriotic, pro-abortion, and anti-life. All of these are ideological dogmatic beliefs, and people have lost their jobs, or their reputations, by publicly disagreeing with them.

In the 21st century there is a new phrase to describe this. It is called Cancel Culture. The idea behind Cancel Culture is essentially a pubic shaming. Cancel Culture results in a collective attempt to damage your reputation, your livelihood, and any social media presence you may have. It can affect anything of public worth including the reputations of people, products, TV shows, celebrities, and employees. All of this for having violated a particular ideological standard. Essentially, it operates as a mechanism whereby a small number of people can oppress and control a much larger population.

Ideological dogmatism became a tool for a smaller number of people to prepare the French people for the revolution to come. The way this operated was to play off of the dissatisfaction a group felt, and then to enact a culture war as a strategy to place their opponent off balance, usually over something to do with equity. The leaders of the revolution then applied these dogmatic views to this group, and used them to silence any opposition. The result in France was tremendous. You can imagine this happening today. Just think of how the college crowd has fomented dissatisfaction that political groups have used to mix with the dogmatism they are pushing. Using words and phrases like "You are a racist," "You are a homophobe," "You are anti-science," "You are a white nationalist," etc. People in the 21st century are prepared to accept only one way of thinking. The ideas being pushed by the dogmatists.

In the 20th century every communist revolution followed this pattern in which one group was pitted against another to foment hatred and dissatisfaction over equity. Using the techniques of Marx, these people pitted the intellectual against the laborer. Owners of capital

Figure 15.

(Business owners) became the exploiters of the people they hired. During the French Revolution it was the dissatisfaction over inequality in governance and the oppressive taxes and fees placed upon an unfranchised and oppressed peasant class that was the glue that held together the philosophic views of the dogmatists. See Figure 15.

They say a picture is worth a thousand words. In Figure 15 we can graphically see what was causing the dissatisfaction of the peasant class prior to the revolution. This lithograph is an actual political cartoon that was produced in France during this period in history. I have enlarged a portion of it and converted it to greyscale so that you can see the three groups that were oppressing the common person in France. Starting from the right we find the first group were the landed nobles. These were the wealthy landowners who rented the properties that the peasants lived on. At a time when the predominant industry was agriculture, the nobles had the means of production, including the land, houses, and in some cases the bridges, roads, and places in villages where trade was made. The peasant class owned nothing, and they were not happy about it. The nobles subjected them to rents and fees to cross a bridge or use a road. Fees could also be charged to trade your goods in the village market. You can see in this lithograph how oppressive this was felt by the peasant class. Notice the chain in the noble's hand as he grasped the poor peasant's neck. The peasant class was truly enslaved to the desires of the wealthy class.

If something similar were to be envisioned today, it would be the seen the desire of the billionaire class to own all the means of production today. You see this on display in the vision of today's World Economic Forum (WEF). This wealthy and connected group imagine the world of the future where you will own nothing and be happy. In order to save the planet, they will provide your housing, your transportation, and they will own the farmland. They will control the market place (think Amazon, PayPal, Mastercard, etc.). They will decide where you live, what you eat, and determine if you can go places. Of course, they will own the means for all of this. They will track your every move and will decide if you qualify for health care, and at what level. It will be a complete authoritarian technocracy.

Moving to the center of the lithograph, we find the wealthy and powerful Roman Catholic Church. The overweight figure of the bishop ruling over this kneeling man, complete with a grimace on his face, is the picture of the wealthy and proud papacy that was the state religion in France. Even though there may have been a few Protestants still left in France, the papacy used the power of the state to mass murder Protestants in a still celebrated

St Bartholomew massacre that took place in 1572. The papacy was the dominant religion, and it was married to the state. At the time of the French Revolution, the people of France paid taxes that went to the papacy, which also owned much property.

Next, on the far left was the government tax collector. This image of the tax man rifling through the personal belonging of a peasant woman brings to mind a recent law in America to hire 87,000 IRS agents. At that time the government was in need of more and more taxes due to the many wars in which France was involved. This constant need further inflamed dissatisfaction in the peasant class, since it was a tax on income as well as sons, who were conscripted to fight the king's battles. The wealthy nobles paid some, but their connections to the monarchy and obligations that entailed, often lessened the taxes that they paid. The bulk fell upon the common people.

To add to the woes of the poor and middle class in France was the system of governance that was seen as disenfranchising the people. At this time France could be likened to a representative monarchy. The king at the time of the French Revolution was Louis XVI. Coming from the line of Bourbon monarchs, he would be the last king of France. Along with the king, the government of France also included three additional groups called the States - General, or three estates. Figure 16 shows the arrangement of the French government prior to the Revolution. This power sharing arrangement between the three estates could be likened to having three votes. The nobles, voting for their interests. The papacy, voting its interests in the ear of the king, and also as a voting member of the general assembly. Lastly, there was everyone else. This was the third estate and it consisted of the representatives of the common people.

The Government of France prior to the revolution

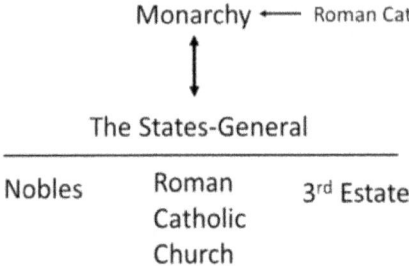

Monarchy ⟵ Roman Catholic Church

↑
↓

The States-General
_____

Nobles   Roman Catholic Church   3rd Estate

Figure 16.

The reason the common people felt disenfranchised was due to the competing interests of the three groups. In order for the third estate to find relief, one of the other groups would have to agree and vote with them. Finally, the king needed to agree as well. This did not happen very often. The result was a one-sided government dominated by the politically connected wealthy, the powerful papacy, and the king. To imagine the extent of the people's dissatisfaction, consider the lithograph in Figure 17.

What a picture of dissatisfaction over equity. On the right you find the fully clothed and overweight clergy of the Roman Catholic Church. In the middle are the nobles. They are depicted as naked, with the exception of a loin cloth, and their fancy hats. This just shows the incredible wealth and power of the papacy compared even to the wealthy class. On the far left was the third estate. Here the common people only have a head, the rest a skeleton, no clothes, no skin, only a skeleton. Interestingly, they are also depicted as being the people who do all the labor (the shovel) and fight the king's wars (the sword).

Figure 17.

Can you imagine a political and social situation today that would spark this kind of dissatisfaction. Once again, the WEF vision for the world will create a system that politically, and practically disenfranchises the common person. It will result in a situation where they have no voice, even with democratically elected representatives. To understand the roots of this system, we need to look at the next set of teachings that were popular during the French Revolution.

COSMOPOLITIANISM – HUMANITARIANISM - PHILOSOPHISM

Imagine for a moment a group of people who are against nation-states. Their desire was for a complete elimination of borders, tariffs, and impediments from governments that would prevent them from taking advantage of the cheapest labor, the most favorable trade, and the least infringement of their ability to produce wealth. They viewed themselves more as a citizen of the world, rather than of a nation state. Now, add to this an attitude, a belief that mankind can perfect himself. It can evolve itself, and there is absolutely no need of divine aid. It is this proud feeling that humanity (or at least the elite within it) are the masters of the universe. Now imagine that this group has developed a new way of communicating with the masses. It uses language in the same way a magician uses a prop to distract the audience from seeing what is really going on. If you can imagine this, then you are living in a world where cosmopolitanism, humanitarianism, and philosophism are becoming dominant in culture and society.

This was certainly part of the attitudes that the leaders of the French Revolution possessed, and it has become a dominant part of life in the 21st century as well. Consider where these attitudes led the rebels during the French Revolution. It led to the rise of an atheistic and autocratic ruler named Napoleon. This proud man who showed the world that humanity rules, crowned himself Emperor by this own hands. His authority came from no higher power than himself. He looked at the nation states of Europe and denied them their sovereignty. He ended their borders, took their stuff, and was intent on making this worldwide -- all for the good of society. We see something similar with Hitler during World War II, and it is evident with the globalist organizations in the world today.

When governments are about to take your stuff, they always use language that is an illusion. Consider the language that is used today in political discourse. They garner support for laws through the use of philosophism. For example, the passage of a law called "The Inflation Reduction Act" which is filled with spending that will only increase inflation on the common person. Another example is the use of the word "equity." This word is often used to sell the people on a law designed to discriminate against a particular group. During the French Revolution, phrases like "bread of equality" were thrown about to justify the nationalizing of business and the taking of lands and houses. These things did little to bring about equity, but they cemented in place the political structure of socialism still present in France today.

One of the byproducts of the French Revolution for future generations were her philosophers. It was French philosophers who sparked a new form of philosophy in the 20th century that became known as postmodernism. Following the teachings of Marx, this philosophy is the ultimate form of philosophism, and is designed to break down authority. Under postmodernism there is no such thing as truth, only truths. This system is a rush to the lowest common denominator as its adherents challenge any authority that prevents them from the basest and most degrading practices. In this anything goes philosophy, a man can be a woman, and vice-versa. A child can become a sexual object, a criminal a victim, and no standard of truth will stand up to the literary illusions, of postmodern methodologies. When you hear someone use words like "critical theory," you are most likely stepping into the illusion they desire to trap you in.

Can you see anything like this happening in your world today. Absolutely. The world of the 21st century is in the midst of its own enlightenment. Technological advances have reached a point where a small number of people can control billions. In the last 20 years we have seen the rise of the information age, the age of discovery in genetics, biology, artificial intelligence, robotics, and nanotechnology. All of these are changing the world. On top of this, all of these advances are being integrated into the intellectual, political, and economic world of the 21st century.

Another major change that is happening in our world is related to how governments and business interact. To illustrate what is happening today, let's compare the way government used to operate 25 years ago with the direction it is going today. See Figures 18 & 19.

About 25 years ago, America and most of the free world had a system of governance that was a free market style of capitalism. At this time government was separate from private business. There was a wall of separation where the citizens would depend upon the government to monitor and regulate the activities of private business to ensure it would not infringe upon the rights of citizens or abuse them in some way. The same thing was present with publicly traded companies.

Government of 25 Years ago
Free Market Capitalism

Wall of Separation

National & Global Corporations   Governments

Shareholders   Citizens

Figure 18.

The boards of these companies were subject to the needs of the shareholders. They were answerable to them, and if they went to far adrift, these CEO's and boards would be voted out. In this system the shareholder had influence to control bad behavior of these corporations. Now, fast forward to the year 2023.

Since the rise of the dominance of the WEF, a new style of governance and market capitalism has arisen. It is called Stakeholder Capitalism. See Figure 19. In Stakeholder Capitalism the implied wall of separation between governments and transnational corporations has been intentionally broken. Elites in government, business, the universities, and entertainment meet to commit themselves to a common cause set by the WEF. This commitment makes them a Stakeholder, and it replaces any commitment to either the citizens who elect them, or the shareholders who enable them. The implied wall of separation is now changed. This Stakeholder relationship insulates the governing official, transnational corporate CEO, or board, from the citizens who elect them, or shareholders who support them. Most people look at this and realize that this relationship is fragile. So, to ensure its success, there is an enabler, a law with a philosophic title – The Patriot Act.

WEF Stakeholder Capitalism
Chinese Style Capitalism

| Transnational & Global Corporations | ⬌ | Governments |

Wall of Separation

Enabler – Patriot Act – Total Surveillance

| Shareholders | | Citizens |

Figure 19.

In 2013 an intelligence contractor named Edward Snowden made a decision that shocked the world and sparked a cold war. Snowden removed a trove of documents that revealed the existence of secret and wide-ranging information gathering programs by the National Security Agency (NSA). Within this trove of information leaked by journalists at the Guardian and the Washington

Post, the world was aghast at the extent of government spying that included spying on innocent citizens. Nothing and no one, was excluded in this net of surveillance. Every kind of internet or cellular connected device was tapped and compromised. The Patriot Act enabled a secret fascist relationship between government and corporations. In documents titled "The Prism Program" consumers saw how government intelligence services came to businesses like Microsoft, Apple, Google, Facebook, Intel, Verizon, AT&T, and many others to create a backdoor system to spy on their customers. Anything that could be connected to the internet or broadcast on cellular networks received a visit from the FBI informing them that they must secretly enable the government to spy on whoever buys their products or uses their services. From smart devices, to computers, software, social media, cell phones, security cameras, you name it. Everything must be designed to enable government's spying on its citizens.

In the years since this revelation, further consolidation of these information sources has been accomplished. Every aspect of a citizen who uses an internet or cellular connected device provides a history of their locations, their contacts, their associations, their communication, their personality, their politics, their vulnerabilities, their health problems, their sins, their credit worthiness, their financial transactions, and their thoughts. What could go wrong here? The WEF desires to take this to the next level with a digital identification that does publicly what the NSA does secretly. They desire to put your whole life under the microscope of technocratic stakeholders for the purposes of allowing or denying you services in the future.

As you can imagine, this revelation sparked a new cold war. Nations around the world realized that they either need to copy this or they will be subject to the Five Eyes, a conglomerate of the world's English-speaking nations that have come together to enact this total surveillance and share intelligence with one another. Today, most of the world has these types of spying operations with the help of transnational companies.

The reason the WEF's plan for world domination is referred to as Chinese-style-communism is due to the implied connection between business and government. Under communism the government owns the means of production. In China there appears to be some kind of private/public partnership. The Chinese government is inserted into every business in China, while it allows for a certain measure of market capitalism. This has shown itself to be a treasure trove for transnational corporations. The Chinese government supplies cheap labor, and in some cases slave labor, to transnational corporations who then reap a tremendous profit when these products are sold in western nations. A good illustration of this is Apple, Walmart, and others. The Chinese government controls the narrative through this arrangement. These companies are extensions of the communist party and can be used to further its reach and influence. Now, the WEF wants to take this style of governance global.

LET'S PAUSE FOR A MOMENT

I am not saying that the WEF plans are going to succeed, but I do see in them the very type of movement that is depicted in the book of Revelation just prior to the coming of the Lord, a gathering of world leaders led by demonic backed religious forces. How many times have you seen the Pope shilling climate change or the need for the coming together of world governments. The Pope's desire for a one-world religion? It is everywhere today. With the United Nation's theory of man-made global warming and the end-of-the-world philosophism of the climate alarmists, it has taken control in all parts of society. This fanaticism is moving us towards a system that will ultimately disenfranchise voters and shareholders. The whole world witnessed President Biden announce that there is going to be a New World Order and America must lead it. Just as prophecy predicts, the dragon, sea beast, and false prophet will work together to gather world leaders. Clearly, the papacy, and America are united in this, and leading it. Now add to this the king-like authoritarianism that the COVID-19 pandemic enabled and you have a complete picture of these stakeholder political leaders acting like kings for one hour with the beast. If successful, the WEF globalist plan will create a class of peasants that are dependent upon their feudal overlords and responsible to cover the costs of it all. It will create the same level of dissatisfaction over equity that existed prior to the French Revolution.

ALL IT TAKES ARE THE RIGHT CIRCUMSTANCES

The historical date for the start of the French Revolution was the year 1789. In the years just prior a drought and harsh winters had left the people hungry and poor. It was then that King Louis XVI called for a special session of the States-General. The king had a problem. He was heavily in debt due to a recent war and needed an infusion of capital. He had planned to call this special session to address this fiscal need and raise taxes, but this time something amazing occurred. The third estate was in an uproar! Realizing that no business could be done, and having been advised by the other two estates, the king suddenly cancels the session and asks for the people to leave. The representatives of the third estate would have none of it. They swore to stay until their grievances with this government were heard.

At this point King Louis XVI could have used the military to enforce his order, but for some unknown reason he let them stay in session. That would turn out to be a fatal mistake on his part. Finding an opening, the third estate used this momentum to open a session of their own. Finding enough sympathetic votes from the clergy and nobles, the third estate voted to end the old governmental structure. The revolution was just beginning.

The next move was the famous storming of the Bastille castle. The main purpose of the raid was to secure gunpower and the weapons and ammunition necessary to repel the anticipated resistance from the king. This resistance was not forthcoming and it further emboldened the third estate to make its next move and form a new government.

With the old government voted out, the third estate set about to create a new one that was called the National Assembly. Along with the new governmental structure that satisfied their desire for fair representation, they created and voted in the Civil Constitution in 1790. It had many similarities with the constitution generated by the rebels in America during its revolution against England in 1776. An important similarity was the ability of citizens to choose their own religion. It was recorded at this time that the papacy, prone to take offence, held its peace. The nobles, having no support from the Catholic nations, prepared themselves to endure all things, and King Louis XVI simply bowed his head to the new law (Madelin, 166). As the impact of what had just occurred was felt by the country, new players came onto the scene. The new constitution would not last.

A new power center was growing around a political faction called the Jacobin Society. The National Assembly was moved to Paris, and with it some eleven hundred

Jacobin clubmen who were not content to just influence what was happening in the Assembly but were seeking to further their reach in France politically through the clubs of the Society. You could think of them in terms of the labor unions of today. They were composed mostly of tradesmen and artisans, and like the progressive wing of the left in America today, they were socialists. Madelin reports that from 1790 onwards the Jacobins became the master of the Assembly, (Madelin, 118).

Four Jacobins represented the extreme left of the Assembly and stood out in their ability to take control and steer the ship. Among them was the famous Robespierre, who as far as ideological dogmatism was concerned was the "purest of the pure." Seeking for the utopia of equality, this group would be the driving force behind the elimination of the Assembly and the remaking of the government once again. Eventually this became something called the Commune. It was described like this by one observer: "When the people puts itself into a state of insurrection; It withdraws all powers and takes them to itself" (Madelin, 267). To add to the troubles of the common person in France, this group began a campaign of philosophism, with slogans like "no wealth-no poverty" and "the bread of equality" as an excuse to nationalize raw materials and privately owned workshops. Doing this further discouraged farmers to produce and caused even greater suffering for this nation. Mob rule was rising and soon it would be directed by Robespierre through an event known as The Terror.

As you might imagine, not everyone who voted to establish the National Assembly, now in ruins, was happy with the direction the left was taking the country. So, to solidify support, the left began a campaign of killing the opposition. At first, it was priests or suspected persons.

However, when a Committee of Surveillance was created, the order was given for the massacre to begin. These killings were justified by philosophism. Calling them enemies of the people, proclaiming that it is an act of justice, the moment had arrived to urge the nation to adopt measures necessary to the Public Safety (Madelin, 287).

The forming of the Committee on Public Safety ensured that more bloodshed would occur. It was said that the country lied under the knife of Robespierre and Danton. Civil war was upon the nation once again, and the left was intent to prevail. A Giant Assembly was held. In this process, the left was able to mark out the opposition, including King Louis XVI, who would shortly be declared guilty and executed. Measures for "public safety" were enacted and a *Revolutionary Tribunal* was formed, all of this leading to the establishment of the Committee of Public Safety, which would serve as the shadow government to root out and kill all detractors.

Public Safety became the cry that battered the revolution weary nation. A new device that had been created to ensure equity was being put to use. It was observed that the rich die more quickly than the poor, who were hanged. This needed to be fixed, and an invention by a man named Guillotine was seen as the solution. It was put to use with a fervor. A Grand Inquisitor was sanctioned to be the public prosecutor, and Robespierre assured the masses that all this blood spilt was necessary in service to the law. This is where cancel culture leads, when given the power to do so. It was said that the Terror ended when Robespierre himself was put on the guillotine. See Figure 20 for a depiction of Robespierre and The Terror.

Figure 20.

ANTI-CHRISTIANISM & CLASSICISM

Two other university teachings were also present in the revolution. The first was a spirit of classicism. This is the desire for the past glory and culture of the Greek and Roman empire. Add to this the belief that Christianity is bad for society, and you have a picture of the feelings of the left. In the midst of the revolution, they began to move on these beliefs and ended Christianity in France. This period of dechristianization lasted about three and a half years (See Revelation 11:7-12). Just as the prophecy in Revelation 11 indicated, France became a place of immorality (Sodom) and unbelief (Egypt). In such a short time, the world witnessed the rise of the beast from the bottomless pit.

Dechristianization began first by the confiscation of church property, including the extensive papal lands. Churches were looted, and then repurposed. Priests were to forsake Rome and were told to get married. To solidify the atheistic desires, the days of the week were expanded to ten to hide the creation week, and the calendar times and names changed. A year zero was proclaimed in rebellion of a dating system that begins with the birth of Christ. The items of superstition in Roman Catholic worship and dress were tossed to the floor of the Assembly and in the streets, as a mockery of the entire system. A good way to discern the sentiments of the times would be to consider the popular posters of the day such as seen in Figure 21.

Figure 21 shows two posters with a very common theme during the Revolution. There were many to choose from. Some have a more Roman style, such as the bundle of sticks tied together with a serpent wrapped around it, as seen on the right. This common Roman symbol is an illustration of how people bound to a common cause can become a deadly weapon for change.

LA RAISON

Figure 21.

The woman in both is titled "The Reason." In the picture on the left she holds in her left hand the all-seeing-eye, common in Luciferian mystery cults as well as on the US one dollar bill. The all-seeing-eye is found on top of the bundle of sticks in the picture on the right. In both of them, Reason grasps a lion by the mane. This symbolism reveals the ethos of the beast who rises out of the abyss. Human reason, guided by mystical insight, can conquer and tame the pesky Lion of the tribe of Judah – Jesus.

The most famous part of this age of reason, were the events taking place at the Catholic cathedral Notre Dame. Here a celebration of Reason was held with an actress acting as the goddess being carried to the place where the priests would ply their trade. It was proclaimed to be the Temple of Reason, and was a big party, with sexual acts taking place all along the recesses of the building. Another church was repurposed and named The Pantheon. It was to house monuments to the great leaders of the revolution. It still stands in Paris today as a museum displaying the triumph of secularism and human achievement. The beast has ascended and the world has been taken over by its Luciferian flavor. Reason after all, has been called "Man's imitation of divinity" by one modern philosopher. Here in the French Revolution, it was born and took roots.

The pinnacle moment in the dechristianization of France came when the government made a proclamation that "God is not the Creator, and the Bible is not to be followed anymore." Ellen G. White, writing about this time, relays a quote from a contemporary magazine which highlights the historical significance. "France is the only nation in the world concerning which the authentic record survives, that as a nation she lifted her hand in open rebellion against the Author of the universe. Plenty of blasphemers, plenty of infidels, there have been, and still continue to be, in England, Germany, Spain, and elsewhere; but France stands apart in the world's history as the single State which, by the decree of her legislative assembly, pronounced that there was no God, and of which the entire population of the capitol, and a vast majority elsewhere, women as well as men, danced and sang with joy in accepting the announcement" (The Great Controversy, The Bible and the French Revolution).

History reveals that at the end of this three and a half years of terror, the French people, worn out by the horrors the political left hoisted upon them, cried out for relief. That relief came through the rise of an autocratic ruler named Napoleon. A man who became beloved in France, who once again legalized religion, and restored the nation by putting down the Jacobins. Napoleon rose to power, crowned himself Emperor, and then took the revolution to its final act -- world domination.

To close this topic, I would like to share a picture of the revolution from the perspective of France's neighbors looking on. This is how the people in England saw what was happening in France during the Terror and dechristianization periods. See Figure 22.

[10] And those who dwell on the earth will rejoice over them, make merry, and send gifts to one another, because these two prophets tormented those who dwell on the earth.
Revelation 11:10

Figure 22.

In this picture, which is titled "The Radicals Arms," we see the shocking scene that existed in France. At the top you have the hat of the Jacobin surrounded by the axes that killed so many of their own citizens. This is flanked by the noose, and in the center, we find the final solution the guillotine. The blade of the guillotine has the symbols of what was killed, monarchy, papacy, Christ. Surrounding these, a man and woman celebrating in a drunken stupor while trampling underfoot the Bible, and, along with it, the superstitious relics of the papal church. What is most striking is what you find in the center. A world on fire!

Now, I want you to imagine this same thing happening on a worldwide stage. The dragon, beast, and false prophet gathering the leaders of the earth to come together for a final battle against our Creator. Unbeknownst to them, God has put in the heart of the 10 horns to accomplish their desires. In one hour, this union is united, Armageddon occurs. The secular red beast filled with names of blasphemy turns on the apostate Babylon. She is burned with fire, as are all who cling to her. Babylon is fallen. A final proclamation is heard, "God is not the Creator of life, and the Bible is not to be followed anymore. A final indignation and end of religion on the earth. Let your mind imagine what you see in Figure 16, happening around the world. A World on Fire!

PROPHETIC NOTE:

Ellen G. White (1827-1915) was a Christian author and prophetic voice in the 19th and early 20th century. She wrote multiple volumes on practical Christianity, Bible exposition, and prophecy. She wrote in the late 19th century these words regarding the influence of the French Revolution. "The world-wide dissemination of the same teaching that led to the French Revolution – all tend to involve the whole world in a struggle similar to that which convulsed France" – (Education, page 228.) There is no question that this is true today, and is advancing throughout the world.

Chapter 9

What a Christian Should Do Now.

It is easier to see the fulfillment of Bible prophecy in hindsight. When the events have not taken place, one needs to avoid being dogmatic. That is the approach I am taking. However, having said that, there is plenty of reason to map what the Revelation reveals about the course the world is taking. Will you be prepared if what I have shown you is correct? What should a Christian take away from these chapters.

First, assess your influence. If you have influence, let your light shine! If you have been waiting for the right moment to share the gospel with your friends, family, coworkers, neighbors, do it now. Do not let this window of opportunity pass. In Matthew 24:14 Jesus said that the gospel will go to the whole world, and then the end will come. Praise God that you have influence to be a part of this great work. If your influence to share the gospel is weak, try literature evangelism. As long as people have access to online Christian programming, then point people to the ones that prepare them to meet Jesus. Use whatever avenue you have to point people to their great need of our Savior Jesus.

Second, remember what the Lord said about the popularity of biblical Christianity when the end comes. "And you will be hated by all for My name's sake. But he who endures to the end shall be saved" (Mark 13:13). In another place Jesus indicates that before His coming He will be rejected by this generation (Luke 17:25). Therefore, don't be surprised when you begin to see biblical Christian influences fade like a fire that is about to go out. You will know the end is near, and that God is preparing to pour out the seven last plagues upon the earth. The battle of Armageddon described earlier is really the climax of the efforts that have been in preparation for years to align the world for the end. Long before this time, its structural framework will be built. Maybe you have noticed the rise of socialist governments throughout the world, led by authoritative figures. You might begin to see transnational corporations acting in concert to enact a globalist agenda. You could notice that world governments are wondering after the papacy. What should you plan for?

One important thing you may want to consider is how you will conduct commerce when the government requires the financial system to freeze you out? This has already happened in Canada, when the truckers protested the mandatory Covid shot. It has happened in Brazil against people protesting the shady election of a socialist into the presidency in 2022. More and more we watch as access to financial services are closed for individuals who have the nerve to speak out against the popular dogma. Learning to live in a barter economy may be the only way to survive a time when you refuse to worship the beast, or its image, or take its mark, or the number of its name.

Third, read the book of Jeremiah. Jeremiah was the prophet when the end came for God's people. Just as we find in Revelation 12 and 13, there was a remnant who were obedient to God's commands, and there was the religious majority who were unwilling to hear the prophetic warning of Jeremiah. You might know someone like them who says "He will do nothing, no disaster will come upon us, nor shall we see sword or famine" (Jeremiah 5:12-13, ESV). Consider what Peter says about such thinking:

> 3 Knowing this first, that there shall come in the last days scoffers, walking after their own lusts, 4 And saying, Where is the promise of his coming? for since the fathers fell asleep, all things continue as *they were* from the beginning of the creation (2 Peter 3:2–4, KJV).

Do you know someone like this? It would be best to be alert, and walk in the day, for darkness comes when no man can work.

Fourth, don't forget that life will appear to go on like it always has. Remember what Jesus said about the end.

> And as it was in the days of Noah, so it will be also in the days of the Son of Man: 27 They ate, they drank, they married wives, they were given in marriage, until the day that Noah entered the ark, and the flood came and destroyed them all. 28 Likewise as it was also in the days of Lot: They ate, they drank, they bought, they sold, they planted, they built; 29 but on the day that Lot went out of Sodom it rained fire and brimstone from heaven and destroyed *them* all (Luke 17:26–29, NKJV).

During the French Revolution life went on, even during the peak of the horror and killings. People then were marrying and going out to eat and drink. They were planting, and building, buying, and selling. All of us have this ingrained desire for sameness. We fight against anything that disrupts the normal, and in the end, there will be normal things happening all the way until the Lord interrupts this with His coming. The key is to be like the sons of Issachar who had understanding of the times, to know what Israel ought to do (1 Chronicles 12:32).

Fifth, do not despise prophetic utterance, prove all things, and hold fast to what is good (1 Thessalonians 5:20-21). The word despise translates a Greek word that means that you are treating something with scorn so as to discourage people, just as the popular religion in Jeremiah's day. A person who despises prophetic utterance is one who acts as a scoffer to kill this witness in the hearts of others. Do not let yourself be taken in by last day scoffers, because they will be many. Instead, do what Paul suggests: prove what they say, and test it with the Bible. Then hold fast to those things. One of the characteristics of God's remnant in Revelation 12:17 is that they have the gift of prophecy (the Testimony of Jesus). It would be wise at this time to heed what is good, that you may prosper and be a blessing to others. Ellen White is an example of a prophetic voice for the last days. Her book, The Great Controversy, is a good choice to read for today. For example, she writes that the destruction of Jerusalem is a type for the destruction that will take place in the last days.

> The Saviour's prophecy concerning the visitation of judgments upon Jerusalem is to have another fulfillment, of which that terrible desolation was but a faint shadow. In the fate of the chosen city, we may behold the doom of a world that has rejected God's mercy and trampled upon His law. Dark are the records of human misery that earth has witnessed during its long centuries of crime. The heart sickens, and the mind grows faint in contemplation. Terrible have been the results of rejecting the authority of Heaven. But a scene yet darker is presented in the revelations of the future.

The records of the past, —the long procession of tumults, conflicts, and revolutions, the "battle of the warrior ... with confused noise, and garments rolled in blood" (Isaiah 9:5), —what are these, in contrast with the terrors of that day when the restraining Spirit of God shall be wholly withdrawn from the wicked, no longer to hold in check the outburst of human passion and satanic wrath! The world will then behold, as never before, the results of Satan's rule (The Great Controversy Between Christ and Satan, pp 36-37).

She also writes that there will come a time when God's true people will need to flee the cities. This makes sense to anyone living in the 21st century. Our great cities are filled with crime and are like dry leaves waiting for a spark to set them off. There will come a time when they will not be safe for biblical Christians to dwell in. Ellen White writes that there will be a sign when biblical Christians will need to flee these places to avoid persecution. She writes:

The time is not far distant when, like the early disciples, we shall be forced to seek a refuge in desolate and solitary places. As the siege of Jerusalem by the Roman armies was the signal for flight to the Judean Christians, so the assumption of power on the part of our nation, in the decree enforcing the papal sabbath, will be a warning to us. It will then be time to leave the large cities, preparatory to leaving the smaller ones for retired homes in secluded places among the mountains (Last Day Events, 121).

Can you imagine the government making a law that the papal Sunday must be observed? I can. I can see it becoming part of the man-made global warming package. Rest on the Sunday, that you can save the planet.

Unfortunately, it will not be a suggestion at some point. It will become a decree. Honor the papal Sunday! If you are a new covenant Christian, that worships God according to His commandments, this will eventually be a problem.

Related to this, Ellen White counsels believers living in rural and far out places to use this time of relative peace to prepare to receive refugees. In a testimony to the church, she writes this:

> Years ago, I was shown that God's people would be tested upon this point of making homes for the homeless; that there would be many without homes in consequence of their believing the truth. Opposition and persecution would deprive believers of their homes, and it was the duty of those who had homes to open a wide door to those who had not. I have been shown more recently that God would specially test His professed people in reference to this matter. Christ for our sakes became poor that we through His poverty might be made rich. He made a sacrifice that He might provide a home for pilgrims and strangers in the world seeking for a better country, even an heavenly. Shall those who are subjects of His grace, who are expecting to be heirs of immortality, refuse, or even feel reluctant, to share their homes with the homeless and needy? (Testimonies for the Church, Vol. 2, pp. 27–28).

In a small rural church in southern Oregon, I met a woman who told me that the Lord spoke to her and she was told to prepare the church to receive people in need. Her little church took this to heart and brought in a shipping crate and filled it with cots, sleeping bags, and supplies. They bought a fireplace for the fellowship hall and have been updating the church. They saw that God has a purpose for this little church way back in the country.

Finally, don't walk into it. The Bible counsels the wise saying: "A prudent man foresees evil and hides himself, But the simple pass on and are punished" (Proverbs 22:3, NKJV). I don't believe that God wants us to put on our swords and fight the very movements that He Himself is shepherding to bring all things to an end. Instead, it will be a time of discernment, and the need to recognize that God cares for you. As the prophet writes: "Come, my people, enter your chambers, And shut your doors behind you; Hide yourself, as it were, for a little moment, Until the indignation is past (Isaiah 26:20, NKJV). Now is the time to pay attention, to fight back the belief that anything will ever change. Now is the time to know God and be covered by the blood of the Lamb. Now is the time to watch and be faithful. It is my prayer that you may be blessed in these things. May God bless you!

List of Figures

End Notes

A special thanks to George R. Knight for volunteering his time and expertise in editing this manuscript. Thank you so much!

Bibliography

Arndt, W., Danker, F. W., Bauer, W., & Gingrich, F. W. (2000). In _A Greek-English lexicon of the New Testament and other early Christian literature_ (3rd ed., p. 725). University of Chicago Press.11

Brown, Harold, O.J. (2000). _Heresies - Heresy and Orthodoxy in the History of the Church_; Hendrickson Publishers Inc, Peabody, MA.

Doukhan, Jacques B., (2000). _Secrets of Daniel – Wisdom and Dreams of a Jewish Prince in Exile_; Review and Herald Publishing Association.

Madelin, Louis; (1930). _The French Revolution_; William Heinemann LTD; London.

Shea, William H. (1996). _Daniel 7-12 – The Abundant Life Bible Amplifier_; Pacific Press Publishing Association.

Sandeen, Ernest R. (1970). _The Roots of Fundamentalism – British and American Millenarianism_ 1800-1930; The University of Chicago Press, Chicago and London

White, E. G. (1911). _The Great Controversy Between Christ and Satan_; Pacific Press Publishing Association.

White, E. G. (1992). _Last Day Events_ ; Pacific Press Publishing Association.

White E. G. (1855). _Testimonies for the Church_; Pacific Press Publishing Association.